The COMPLETE BEGINNER'S GUIDE *to* GREENHOUSE GARDENING

*A Month-by-Month Planting Book
to Grow 365 Days a Year*

Published by Monkey Publishing
Edited by Emily Hutchinson
Design and Illustrations by Paulo Duelli
Cover Design by Ivica Jandrijevic

Printed by Amazon

1st Edition, published in 2022
© 2022 by Monkey Publishing
Rheinstr. 9
12159 Berlin
Germany
ISBN: 978-3-910282-00-1

TABLE OF CONTENTS

INTRODUCTION

Greenhouse gardening is a rewarding way to grow your own vegetables, herbs and fruits and one that I hope you will enjoy as much as I do. The best thing about a greenhouse is that you don't need a patch of land in order to grow amazing crops. It can be as small and simple as you like or as complex as you can imagine.

By definition, a greenhouse is a structure within which you grow plants. It consists of a frame covered by a transparent glazing, such as glass or plastic sheeting. Greenhouses use the sun to create a warm, beneficial, growing environment. They also protect plants from the elements, pests, diseases, and allow for longer growing seasons. There are many types of greenhouse structures. They are categorized by the amount of additional heat they provide and then further categorized by the actual type of structure.

Greenhouse-like structures go back to the days of the Romans. During cold weather, Roman gardeners stored vegetable plants under frames covered in an oiled cloth. They also planted vegetables in carts that could be moved outside during the day and inside at night to protect them. There are texts from 15th century Korea describing greenhouses designed to manage temperature and humidity for optimal plant growth. Greenhouses became known in parts of Europe in the 17th century. These early greenhouses took a lot of effort to manage. Balancing the heat was a huge problem and closing them up at night or winterizing them was complicated. Charles Lucien Bonaparte, a French botanist in the early 1800s, is said to have created the first modern greenhouse. These greenhouses were called orangeries since they were mainly used to protect orange trees from harsh, freezing temperatures. Greenhouse design continued to develop during the 17th century in Europe, but the Victorian Era is when they really began to take off. They were often elaborate structures built for the wealthy to showcase their gardens.

Since then, greenhouses have become a common sight in home gardens. Their size, design, shape, and function have changed and adapted through the years, and still today, there are new innovations for better, more efficient and effective greenhouses. Most recently, the availability of polyethylene film, or heavy plastic sheeting, has radically changed how greenhouses are built. Previously, they were almost exclusively built using glass, which works well but has limitations, such as its fragility. The introduction of PVC pipe and lightweight aluminum frames has also significantly changed greenhouse building.

The main purpose of most greenhouses, especially if they are cold-frames, is to get an early start on the growing season. This means that it gets used as an interim stage before seedlings are actually placed in the garden. Many vegetables can be started in your house or other inside location under grow lights and when they're big enough, they can be moved out to the greenhouse. Once the outside temperature is warm enough, they can then be planted in the garden. Peppers and tomatoes can be started as early as January or February inside when they have a greenhouse to relocate to after they have begun growing. This means they will be ripe a month or so before any similar plants grown without a greenhouse. Greenhouses are also used to grow plants all year round in a controlled environment. They are closed off from the elements which makes them perfect incubators for many plants. Another popular reason for using a greenhouse is to grow fruits and vegetables in the cold winter months. This usually requires a heated greenhouse, yet there is some flexibility, and a lot can depend on the temperature where it is located.

Chapter 1
_____

TYPES OF GREENHOUSES

IS IT A GREENHOUSE OR A COLD FRAME?

Overview of different types of Greenhouses.

A professional greenhouse builder or gardener might take issue with what is being called a greenhouse. The term greenhouse, to most people, means a structure that holds plants and protects them from the elements while encouraging good growing conditions. A seasoned greenhouse user or a professional gardener, however, makes a very important distinction as to what constitutes a greenhouse and what doesn't.

Simply put, a greenhouse is a structure that has the means to provide internal heat. Any structure that does not have that ability is a cold frame. Cold frames provide protection, yet do not have any heating systems, relying almost exclusively on that which comes naturally from the sun.

An easy way to think of it is that a real greenhouse has a heating system installed that can run year-round if needed. It heats the entire greenhouse and keeps a consistent temperature. A cold frame doesn't have such a system installed. This doesn't mean a cold frame is without heating options. Frost covers, heat mats, cloches, portable heaters, and bubble wrap are all tools available for the cold frame greenhouse. These devices provide a small amount of heat, usually in a very concentrated manner and do not heat the entire greenhouse.

In the eyes of professional gardeners, a greenhouse allows the gardener to control the temperature and environment in ways that aren't possible with a cold frame. In this definition of greenhouses, there are three types: hothouse, warm house, and cool house. The difference between these three types lies in where it is located and the temperature maintained inside it. A hothouse has a minimum temperature of 60°F. A warm house has a minimum temperature of 55°F, and a cool house has a minimum temperature of 45°F. The key to these designations, and what sets them apart from cold frames is that the temperature is controlled and maintained throughout the entire greenhouse.

A greenhouse that grows plants year-round in a cold climate will need to have supplemental heating. The type of greenhouse heating that you need will depend on your climate and what you are growing. In places with a mild climate, you may only need to provide a little heating, or even none at all. Growing tomatoes, cucumbers, flowers and tropical plants will require a hothouse in places where the temperature gets quite low. A location with warm seasonal weather year-round can grow these same vegetables and flowers in a cold frame, using only the sun as heat. A greenhouse structure can be a cold-frame in the summer when the sun is sufficient for heating. Then, in winter, it can be turned into a hothouse or warm house to grow plants regardless of the temperature outside.

Many cold frame structures cannot be turned into real greenhouses, even if heat is added. Lack of proper ventilation for a heated space is a huge consideration. If the structure is small, any added heat can cook the delicate plants. Cold frame structures with single-pane glass, plastic sheeting, or polycarbonate windows do not provide any insulation. Any heat that is added will quickly dissipate, negating its addition in the first place. This gets confusing though, because the term cold frame is also used to describe a certain type of structure. According to professional gardeners, a hoop house is a type of cold frame, as is a low tunnel and often a dome as well. An attached greenhouse, A-frame, or traditional style can be a cold frame or have heating to make it a greenhouse.

To the average gardener, this is confusing, and so in this guide, we will try to keep it simple. We will continue defining a greenhouse as any structure that holds plants. Just be aware that not everyone identifies it like this.

If you are looking into purchasing a greenhouse, a great way to decipher whether you are looking at a greenhouse or cold frame is to ask where a ventilation fan can be installed. A cold frame will not have a place for a ventilation fan to be permanently installed. Another great tell is the price. Greenhouses that provide internal heat are a lot more expensive, generally never less than $1,000.

COLD FRAME

A cold frame provides protection for the plants from the physical elements, like snow, rain, storms and frost. However, it doesn't have any additional heating installed, so if the outside temperatures are low or freezing, then the plants will freeze as well. Cold frame structures can still take advantage of frost covers, heating pads and other measures to help their seedlings along.

Cold frame structures are used a lot in the springtime to house plants before they are planted in a garden. They act as an in-between to harden the plants off. Seedlings that have been started inside a house cannot go straight from that environment out to the garden. They need a week or so to gradually acclimate to the change in temperature and the elements. Once the outside temperature is above freezing, a cold frame greenhouse can be used to start seedlings. The heat from the sun during the day keeps it warm enough for the seeds to sprout and flourish.

A cold frame greenhouse can also be beneficial in the fall to extend the growing season. When the temperatures outside are starting to get really cool, the heat from the sun is still enough to keep the plants growing for a while.

Plants can be put right in the ground and covered with a cold frame structure as well. Even in the winter, the heat from the sun during the day is often enough for some plants to thrive.

Cold frame structures are usually only good for two-three weeks in the spring and then another two-three weeks in the fall. Their use is limited in many ways; however, in climates where those two-three weeks make a big difference in plant growth, they are extremely useful. For the minimal expense of building such a structure, the reward can be quite great.

Since gardeners are generally an adventurous type, there has been lots of experimentation using cold frames to grow plants throughout the winter. See the section on winter gardening for more information.

COLD FRAME GREENHOUSE

Ideal for springtime to house plants.

This type of greenhouse is placed directly in the garden. It is small and portable, so it can be moved around to accommodate different sets of plants.

Cold frame greenhouses are greenhouse building at its simplest. A sheet of plastic anchored over the plants in the garden is the easiest cold frame structure. A cold frame structure is most often a box with a hinged lid. The lid has transparent windows, usually made with glass. Recently, polycarbonate has been a popular choice because it doesn't break as easily as glass. Shattered glass in a garden is not something anyone likes to deal with.

This is as low-tech as it gets with minimal effort expended. The cost to create a cold frame greenhouse is small and can be as simple as

THESE TYPES OF GREENHOUSES ARE USED IN THE SPRING AND FALL TO EXTEND GROWING SEASONS.

buying plastic sheeting. The type of structure you build is completely dependent on your budget. This is a favorite choice among DIY gardeners since it is so adaptable and easy to create.

These types of greenhouses are used in the spring and fall to extend growing seasons. In the spring, they can help seedlings to stay warm and help them grow before they would normally be planted outside. The sun heats the plastic or glass, keeping the ground and plants warm underneath the covering. There needs to be ventilation in case it gets too hot, and the common method for ventilating cold-frames is propping up the door of the structure. It is possible to cook the plants if they aren't checked often. This is the biggest downside to this type of structure as it is quite easy to overheat the plants with a cold frame structure.

It is common to see old pallets being re-used as a frame. Old window frames are also a common choice. Cold frames are a great starter greenhouse. They range in size, and you can buy one pre-made or make one yourself.

HOOP GREENHOUSE (HIGH TUNNEL)

Ideal to harden off new plants

Hoop greenhouses are becoming very popular among gardeners. They consist of a heavy sheeting plastic draped over a long-arched frame. The frame is usually made of PVC pipe or wire. They are well-liked for their versatility. They can be a permanent structure, secured to the ground and covering the crops in your garden, they can be attached to a raised bed or built to be portable.

High tunnel greenhouses are almost the same in construction to hoop houses; however, they are usually made with a steel frame and can be much bigger and longer. Many have roll-up side walls to help with ventilation. Also, in a high tunnel greenhouse, the plants grow in raised beds instead of directly in the ground.

A hoop house is similar in function to a cold frame structure; however, its design is different, and it

THE MAIN PURPOSE OF BOTH TYPES OF STRUCTURES IS TO HARDEN OFF NEW PLANTS AND PROVIDE EXTRA TIME IN THE GROWING SEASON.

uses different materials. Neither of them has additional heating, and both are limited as to what they can do. The main purpose of both types of structures is to harden off new plants and provide extra time in the growing season. The pros are that they are easy to build and easy to adapt for size and location. Snow and rain slide easily off the roof because of the curved shape. They are inexpensive compared to many other designs.

They are not as sturdy as an A-frame or post and beam structure. In places with high winds, a hoop house will have to be very carefully secured, and they may not be an option at all in some areas.

LOW TUNNEL

Simple in design and inexpensive to build.

A low tunnel greenhouse is a mini hoop greenhouse. It has a rigid structure of pipe bent into an arc over the garden rows and is generally covered with row cover material or plastic. It only stands about 2'-3' high. It covers the crops in the garden just enough to protect them from the elements and pests. A caterpillar tunnel is larger, usually about 6'-8' high and 10'-20' wide. They are held in place in the garden over the vegetables with ropes and stakes.

The main difference between these types of greenhouses and a hoop house is that they are removed from the garden when not in use. They are much simpler in design and less expensive to build or buy. They are also less durable and will most likely have to be replaced on a semi-frequent basis.

WHEN THE SUN IS OUT, THE PLANTS ARE RECEIVING THE LIGHT FULLY. WHEN YOU ARE GROWING IN THE EARLY SPRING, OR EVEN WINTER, THIS MAKES A HUGE DIFFERENCE TO THE SUCCESS OF YOUR GARDEN.

The function of low tunnels and caterpillar tunnels is similar to cold frame greenhouses in that they offer protection against the elements and not much else. The biggest difference, and it's a big one, is in its design. A cold frame structure has walls and edges and a frame that blocks light from entering. Low tunnel greenhouses have no wall or roof, so when the sun is out, the plants are receiving the light fully. When you are growing in the early spring, or even winter, this makes a huge difference to the success of your garden.

Low tunnel greenhouses are also larger than cold frames. This means you can grow a larger harvest, or you can start a lot more crops earlier. Low tunnels are also lighter in weight and can be moved around your garden space more easily.

Like hoop houses, low tunnel and caterpillar greenhouses need to be secured well, or they can be blown away. They are not always an option for places with high winds.

ATTACHED GREENHOUSE (LEAN-TO)

Benefits from existing resources.

This type of greenhouse shares a wall with an existing structure, hence the name 'attached'. Often, they are built onto the south-facing side of a house. They are also often attached to sheds, barns, and garages. They can be large or small, taking up the whole side of your house or just a small portion of your porch or deck.

The benefits of sharing a wall with an existing structure are many. Construction costs are generally lower than stand-alone structures since there is one wall already in place. Heat, water, and electricity are usually nearby and easily accessible. This is very practical and eliminates a lot of initial stress about providing heat for your plants and how to water them. They need to be watered every day, so if getting water to them is an issue, it can be overwhelming. The

THE BENEFITS OF SHARING A WALL WITH AN EXISTING STRUCTURE ARE MANY. CONSTRUCTION COSTS ARE GENERALLY LOWER THAN STAND-ALONE STRUCTURES SINCE THERE IS ONE WALL ALREADY IN PLACE.

8th principle of Permaculture states, "Integrate rather than segregate." In this situation, having your plants next to your living space helps you to integrate their care into your daily life and routine. It becomes less of a burden to look after them, the less you need to travel to get to them. The main downside to an attached greenhouse is that it may become hard to regulate the temperature inside. The wall that the greenhouse shares with the other structure may collect the sun's heat. Also, the sun can only come from three sides, limiting the plant's exposure to light. An attached greenhouse is generally constructed with glass windows. Recently, however, some greenhouse kits are using twin-wall polycarbonate glazing panels because they are less expensive and do a good job.

A window-mounted greenhouse is a type of attached greenhouse that is built into the window frame of a house. These are small and compact. They can be attached so that they can be accessed from inside, outside or both.

DOME GREENHOUSE

Uses space effectively.

Dome greenhouses get their name from their shape: they are shaped like a dome. The frame is made up of triangulated sections with plastic sheeting covering them. This means that there is no separate roof or walls; it is all one surface with light coming in from all directions.

These types of greenhouses have a lot of great benefits. They are lightweight, sometimes portable, and stable in wind and snow. The strength of the triangle frame makes it sturdier than many other greenhouses. There are no internal supports, and the triangles distribute the weight of the frame evenly throughout. Dome greenhouses are reported to survive earthquakes, tornadoes, and hurricanes. In wind storms, the air flows around the shape of the dome instead of pushing against it. In areas

THE STRENGTH OF THE TRIANGLE FRAME MAKES IT STURDIER THAN MANY OTHER GREENHOUSES.

where snow accumulation is an issue, these greenhouses are great. The snow slides easily off the curved structure, unlike a rectangular structure, where the snow will build up on top of it

The biggest draw to this design is the space. The shape of the dome allows the space to be maximized for growing; vertical gardening can be achieved in the space too. The curved dome also maximizes exposure from the sun, which makes it an ideal greenhouse. With this type of structure, it isn't necessary to seek out a south-facing position.

Dome greenhouses also use energy and circulate air more efficiently. The surface area of a building dictates its heat loss, and with the dome, the round surface is significantly smaller than traditional rectangular structures.

The cost of building a dome greenhouse depends on the materials you use. They can be built quite inexpensively. If you decide to build your own, search online for a "dome calculator." These programs let you enter your desired features and will then generate a diagram for you with the correct angles and dimensions.

A-FRAME

Simplicity and ease of assembly.

The allure of this design is its simplicity and relative ease of assembly. An A-frame is shaped like a large tent. It doesn't use as many materials as some of the other greenhouse types. A-frame greenhouses are generally built with glass windows or walls.

The biggest downside is that because the walls narrow, the usability of the space is limited. Also, there can be issues with air-circulation in the four corners.

TRADITIONAL GREENHOUSE (POST AND RAFTER)

Strong and dependable.

This design, along with the A-Frame style, is the most popular choice for greenhouses. The post and rafter greenhouse is strong and dependable. The rafters provide great support to the roof, and the design of the walls makes it easy to utilize all the space inside efficiently. The air circulation is good in this type of structure as well.

Because it is top heavy, this type of greenhouse must be footed, which is an additional expense and construction that you won't need with an A-frame.

HALF-BRICK GREENHOUSE

Bricks retain the heat and help to regulate temperature.

Years ago, greenhouses with a brick foundation were very popular because, with a brick base, not as much glass was needed to complete the greenhouse. This was good because the glass was expensive. This type of greenhouse went out of style for a while yet recently has begun to make a bit of a comeback because there are some definite benefits to the design besides the lower cost.

Bricks absorb heat. During the day, when the sun is shining down, the brick base takes in the heat and prevents the inside of the greenhouse from getting too hot. The bricks retain the heat from the day which helps to keep the temperature of the interior stable during the night and not drop too low. Secondly, these greenhouses look good. They complement your garden aesthetically in ways that other greenhouses don't.

GOTHIC GREENHOUSE

Water and snow run off the roof easily.

The signature design of a gothic greenhouse is its curved roof. It has a semicircular frame, like half of a teardrop, that is usually covered in plastic sheeting. The technique used in building this type of greenhouse makes structural trusses unnecessary. In addition, fewer construction materials are needed which reduces costs.

The benefit to this design stems from its unique shape. Water and snow run off the roof easily, and it can withstand strong winds and heavy snow. Also, it conserves heat nicely. However, the downside of this design is also related to the shape. While the center of the greenhouse is tall under the arch, which is great for tall plants, the low side walls limit the planting space.

PIT GREENHOUSE

Increased protection from the elements.

This type of greenhouse is built largely underground. The interior of the greenhouse is below ground while the roof is above ground. The roof has panels of either glass or plastic to provide heat and light, like any other greenhouse. The inside walls can be built of stone, mud brick, or other material that will absorb heat and keep the greenhouse warm.

In daylight, the earthen walls of the greenhouse store up the heat. At night, they release that heat and keep the interior space warm. Above ground greenhouses only get the benefit of natural heat storage from one side, the ground. Whereas pit greenhouses utilize the four underground walls and the ground itself for heat storage. This type of greenhouse is highly energy efficient.

Another benefit of this type of greenhouse is

IN DAYLIGHT, THE EARTHEN WALLS OF THE GREENHOUSE STORE UP THE HEAT. AT NIGHT, THEY RELEASE THAT HEAT AND KEEP THE INTERIOR SPACE WARM.

increased protection from the elements. The downsides are the cost of digging a trench and building a foundation. Drainage is also an important issue to be considered.

If your property has a high water table, this is obviously not a good choice, or you'll have a flooded greenhouse. A pit greenhouse should be built at a minimum of five feet above the water table.

PORTABLE GREENHOUSE

Lightness and portability.

Several of the options in this list are types of portable greenhouses. Cold frames and hoop houses are often built with the intention of moving them around as needed. However, there is another type of portable greenhouse that is becoming readily available and popular around the world. These greenhouses are usually a wire frame with shelving, covered with plastic, and with some type of entrance. They look like a camping or pop-up tent with shelves inside and transparent covering. Many of them use rope and stakes to secure them to the ground. They come in a variety of sizes, some not more than 4'x6'.

These greenhouses can be found in most garden supply stores and are easily assembled and set up. The upside is their lightness and portability. They can be folded up and stored like a tent

ANOTHER TYPE OF PORTABLE GREENHOUSE THAT IS BECOMING READILY AVAILABLE AND POPULAR AROUND THE WORLD.

each season. When you are ready to set it up, it doesn't take long, and you can choose (and change) where you want it. The downside is that they generally are not that sturdy since they aren't attached to a base. There are options that are more heavy duty than others, so if you are looking for one, make sure to research that.

TYPES OF GREENHOUSES
Comparison

TYPE OF GREENHOUSE					
COST:	$	$	$	$$$	$$
GROWING SEASONS:	1	2	2	4	4
HEATING COST:	$	$$$	$$$	$	$
YEARS OF LIFE:	<3	3-5	<3	10-15	10-15
FOUNDATION:	No	No	No	Yes	Yes-No
STRENGTH OF FRAMEWORK:	⇓⇓	⇓	⇓	⬆⬆	⬆⬆
WIND RESISTANCE:	⇓⇓	⇓	⇓	⬆⬆	⬆⬆
LIGHT:	💡	💡	💡	💡⬆	💡⬆

THE BEGINNER'S GUIDE TO GREENHOUSE GARDENING *Richard Bay*

$$$	$$$	$$$	$	$$	$
3	4	4	3	3-4	2
$$	$	$$	$	$$$	⚡
5-10	10-15	10-15	∞	10-15	<3
Yes-No	Yes	Yes	Yes	Yes-No	Yes
↑	↑	↑	↑↑	↑	↓
↑	↑↑	↑	↑↑	↑	↓
💡	💡	💡↑	💡↓	💡↑	💡↑

THE BEGINNER'S GUIDE TO GREENHOUSE GARDENING *Richard Bay*

Chapter 2

GREENHOUSE PLANNING, CONSTRUCTION & ENVIRONMENT

CONSTRUCTING A GREENHOUSE

There are several ways to build a greenhouse. You can build one yourself if you are handy or know someone who is. Hoop and cold frame greenhouses are not too difficult and can be finished in a day. If the greenhouse you want is large or requires a foundation, you can hire contractors to build it. There are also many greenhouse kits available online and in gardening stores. Some kits require little to no skill to set up while others will need some construction knowledge to install.

When thinking about building or setting up a greenhouse, investigate the building codes for your area. Portable greenhouses, hoop houses, tunnel greenhouses, and small structures likely won't require any special permits. An attached greenhouse or post and rafter probably will.

DIY

Building your own greenhouse is usually the least expensive way to get the exact greenhouse you want. There are multiple places where you can buy greenhouse plans, or you can sketch and construct one of your own design. This is not always the absolute cheapest choice since it depends on what you want to build. Building materials can get expensive. Plus, the time involved in digging and setting up a foundation and doing the actual construction can add up fast. It is usually best if you have assistance when building your own. Some elements of construction can be difficult for one person.

Of course, the biggest benefit of building your own greenhouse is getting the size and style that you want. You could even combine styles if you wanted to and create your own aesthetic. It can also be designed for a specific type of plant. If the place where you are building the greenhouse is tricky or has specific requirements, this may be your only option. Building your own greenhouse will necessitate having some construction experience or the willingness to spend a lot of time researching and learning. As with most other DIY projects, the time involved in researching, designing, setting up, and then building the greenhouse is extensive when compared to buying a kit.

If you want an attached greenhouse or post and rafter structure, it will likely be necessary to hire someone to build it. The benefit to this is that it will be professionally done.

Building hoop houses and tunnel greenhouses is quite simple and can be completed in a short amount of time with a few helping hands. The supplies are generally inexpensive too, making this a rewarding DIY project.

GREENHOUSE KITS

A quick search online may overwhelm you with all the choices for greenhouse kits. There are a plethora of options for size, style, and price. Some only require a simple snapping together of pieces to assemble them, while others will need all kinds of tools and possibly some construction experience. The one you choose may depend on your own construction skills and knowledge.

Be sure to understand exactly what is needed for the assembly before purchasing the kit. It will be frustrating to find the perfect greenhouse, only to be stalled when you get it out of the box because it is too complicated or difficult for your skill level. If possible, ask the manufacturer for a copy of the manual to read before you buy it to ensure you understand it. If the greenhouse build is going to be a weekend project, check with the company to see if they have customer service on the weekend in case you run into a problem.

Check out all the features of the greenhouse before buying. Does it have ventilation? How much floor space is there? How structurally sound is it? Will it withstand weather conditions in your climate? Does it need a foundation? Will it fit in the space you want to put it? Does the greenhouse benefit the plants you intend to grow?

Many greenhouse kit manufacturers allow you to select custom options. Of course, the more specialty choices, the more expensive the greenhouse. Do your research and find the best one for you.

Greenhouse kits range in size and price. Larger greenhouse kits run approximately 8x20 and cost thousands of dollars. Smaller greenhouse kits can be as little as 27"x18" and cost less than $50.

When you get your kit, check for any damage before beginning construction. It will be hard to get the whole kit replaced, or a specific part replaced when you are in the middle of the assembly. Read the instruction manual before starting.

USED GREENHOUSE

Sometimes, plant nurseries sell their old greenhouses, or a property owner may not want a greenhouse on their property anymore and so are looking to get rid of it. It doesn't happen too often, since well-made greenhouses can last a while. Buying a used greenhouse can save you lots of money; however, as with all used goods, it can also be a money pitfall.

Do your research! Ask the owner how it was used and for how long. Assess the greenhouse for damage. If it has plastic sheeting, it will likely need to be replaced. Also, since the greenhouse has already been constructed, it will need to be taken down and moved. This may be quite expensive and complicated depending on the type of greenhouse. Additionally, it is unlikely the owner will still have the manual, so you may have to find one online or do it by best estimation. It is best to buy a greenhouse that you can dismantle yourself before moving it. This way, you can see how it goes together. Buying a greenhouse that is already disassembled could quickly become a nightmare to put back together. Taking pictures of the greenhouse before you dismantle it will be a huge help. Having some construction knowledge will also be extremely useful.

HOW TO SAVE MONEY

by building your greenhouse

The easiest way to save money building a greenhouse is to thoroughly assess all the options beforehand so when you start building; you aren't coming up against any unanticipated scenarios. Making multiple trips to the hardware store is frustrating and time-consuming. Discovering you don't have the right tools, materials, or instructions can cause long, frustrating, delays. Triple check the location, the size, the building method and that you have the necessary help on the day you plan to build.

If you are building from your own design, check around to see what items you already have available that will work in your build. Do you have brick, wood, windows, or plastic left over from other projects that can be used? Ask around friends and family as well to see if they have any leftover building materials you can use.

Throughout the next chapters, I will provide inexpensive options which will save you money in building and running your greenhouse.

PLANNING FOR A GREENHOUSE

In order to decide which greenhouse works best for you, think about the space that you have, what type of plants you intend to grow, and how much money you want to spend. There is no right or wrong greenhouse. The reason there are so many types is that they have evolved to suit many different situations and budgets. A greenhouse can be a long-term investment.

If you choose an attached or A-frame greenhouse, it will be permanent. In this case, it is especially important to consider your long-term goals. Do you plan on growing the same types of plants year after year? Would you like to increase your plantings at some point? It is always best to plan for more space than you think you will need. It is better to have unused space in your greenhouse than not to have enough.

Another benefit of a larger greenhouse is that the inside temperature is easier to manage against temperature extremes. The larger the amount of thermal mass (soil) being warmed during the day, the more residual heat will be available at night to keep the plants warm.

If you are located in a snowy climate, brace your greenhouse for snow accumulation! Snow is heavy. Very heavy. If you have a lightweight greenhouse that doesn't shed snow build-up, it can collapse. Do not underestimate the weight of snow or the damage it can do.

LOCATION

If you are choosing a stand-alone greenhouse, the location should be your priority. It should be located near your garden or even in your garden. There should be access to electricity and water because you will certainly need them both at some point.

Locate your greenhouse where you will use it to its full potential. If it is too out of the way or difficult to get to, the likelihood of it being used fully is lessened.

A place where the greenhouse gets a minimum

six hours of sun is necessary. In places with a cool climate, more than six hours are better. In places with hot climates, a location that provides some shade is preferred, so the plants don't get overheated. The angle of the sun changes throughout the seasons, so keep this in mind when planning your location. If there isn't a place with that much sun each day, consider adding grow lights to make up the difference.

Orient the greenhouse from east to west, so one long side will be facing south and getting the full sun each day. Nearby trees can provide necessary shade during the summer months. Then, in the winter, when they've lost their leaves, the greenhouse will get the full sun which it will need.

Trees also provide a great windbreak. Most greenhouses are lightweight which makes them function as excellent sails during wind storms. The last thing you want is your greenhouse sailing away! A sheltered location that doesn't disrupt the greenhouse's access to the sun too much is ideal.

Ensure that there is adequate drainage around the area where you build.

FOUNDATION

Whether you are building your own greenhouse or assembling one from a kit; it may need a foundation. The exceptions to this are hoop houses, low and high tunnels, portable, and cold frame greenhouses. These types of greenhouses are meant to be used directly in a garden and moved about, so there is no need for a foundation. If you are building a permanent greenhouse, though, you will need to decide on a foundation type and style.

The foundation of the greenhouse should provide anchoring, water drainage, and weed control. It needs to be anchored, so that wind gusts don't flip it over. Water needs to have a way of exiting the greenhouse. If water isn't drained, it will pool up on the greenhouse floor and attract insects, pests and promote disease. Greenhouses are an ideal location for weeds to thrive. The foundation should include measures that will prevent weed growth, otherwise, they will try to sneak in through the foundation and up through the floor. A layer of ground covering under the base will do this well. It must be landscaping weed barrier cloth, which allows water to drain through the fabric. Black plastic or tarp should not be used.

NO FOUNDATION

A greenhouse under 200 sq. ft can get away without having a foundation at all. Placing the greenhouse directly on the ground can have some real benefits, the first of which is how much easier it is. This greenhouse can be anchored to the ground with cable (see the section on securing against the wind) to keep it stable. The place you are putting it should be level. You can keep the ground as soil and plant right into the ground if you like. Alternately, a gravel or stone floor works well.

WOOD

Wood is an inexpensive and simple choice. Natural decay-resistant woods, such as cedar, redwood, and cypress are recommended.

To ensure the wood doesn't rot, chemically treated wood is often recommended; however, plants absorb chemicals, so this can be problematic. A new type of pressure treated wood came on the market 15 years ago that is said to be mostly non-toxic. The plants still leach the chemicals, yet studies say it is so low it is almost undetectable. An oil finish applied to the pressure treated wood can increase safety. It is not recommended to use any treated timber from over 15 years ago.

If you do decide to use pressure treated wood, be sure to clean up any sawdust and wood shavings after building. There are many grades of pressure treated wood; the one you want for maximum durability is the ground-contact grade or whichever your lumber supplier recommends for below grade installation. If you use a different grade, then it will likely rot out fast. Even when using the correct pressure treated wood, anticipate replacing it every 8-10 years.

Alternately, if you can, the wood can be encased in concrete or other material to prevent it from being in contact with the elements and rotting. The copper used in pressure treating is not compatible with aluminum frames as it will corrode the aluminum. A 10-mm thick barrier, minimum, needs to be placed between any pressure treated wood and aluminum.

CONCRETE

A 3" thick concrete slab floor works well in greenhouses. It is convenient, easy to build, and provides a flat, clean surface in the greenhouse. A drainage pipe in the center of the floor, or several spaced around, will need to be added. Water pools easily on this surface. This drain should take water to a gravel pit or use a pipe to transport it well outside the area of the greenhouse. If using a gravel pit underneath the floor for drainage, a minimum of 4" of compacted gravel or stone should be used.

A foundation needs to have footing, which is the point where the building meets the soil. The walls of the greenhouse are less likely to sag or move when there are footers. Not all greenhouses will require a footing. If they do, check with local building codes as there will be requirements regarding this. Attached greenhouses, traditional style, and A-frames will likely need a footing.

FLOOR

The flooring material in your greenhouse is important for many reasons. This is a place where you may spend hours standing and moving around, so it needs to be comfortable and caring for it should be easy. It is not something you want to have to replace often and choosing the right one from the beginning will prevent that. If the floor is uncomfortable and difficult to navigate, the joy of being in your greenhouse will be diminished.

The flooring options also span a range of costs, from basically nothing to very expensive. There is no right or wrong choice. Find the one that suits your needs and budget best.

The greenhouse floor can be made up of many materials. Sand and fine gravel are great because they provide excellent drainage. Limestone gravel is good because it is alkaline. Brick or stone slabs are aesthetically nice and work well, or you can also go down the route of keeping it dirt and using it to plant into.

DIRT/SOIL

This is a nice option because it is simple. It eliminates a lot of work and saves a lot of money. Benches for plants can be set up on the floor, or you can plant directly into the soil. If the greenhouse is intended to harbor your seedlings until they are ready to be planted in your garden, you will not want to plant them directly in the soil.

They will need to be transplanted, so growing containers are necessary. A greenhouse with a dirt floor can have dual uses. It can hold seedling starts during the spring and then once the garden is planted, the greenhouse floor can be planted as well. This extends your growing space and expands the types of plants that can be grown. This option is popular because it utilizes the greenhouse all year long instead of just during the spring.

Additionally, a greenhouse with a dirt floor can be used for winter growing. In this situation, planting the seeds directly into the soil is ideal. The soil will heat up under the sun during the day and warm the plants through the evening. Many other non-dirt floor options can't do this.

The soil in the greenhouse is a rechargeable battery. In the daytime, when the sun is shining at its brightest, the soil heats up and provides warmth in the space. It also stores warmth and energy. During the cooler evening and nighttime hours, the warmth slowly dissipates, like a battery losing its charge. It will take a while for this to happen; the soil doesn't lose its warmth instantly. This gives the plants heat, even when it is very cold outside. As soon as the sun rises, the soil starts to recharge and take in the heat to tide the plants over for the following night.

The biggest downside to dirt floors is they get muddy when wet. And in a greenhouse, the floor is sure to get muddy with some frequency. It can happen after you've watered your plants. If your greenhouse is located in a low spot, water can seep through the foundation. A soggy, boggy floor is not pleasant to walk on or to work in. To prevent this as much as possible, choose your greenhouse site carefully and make sure it is at a high point on your property, if possible. Carefully water your plants to avoid making too much ending up on the floor. While this may take more time, it is worth it to prevent a muddy mess.

STONE, PAVERS, GRAVEL

Gravel or crushed stone is an inexpensive choice that suits a greenhouse well. It is easy to install, easy to clean and drains excellently. It can provide extra humidity in your greenhouse if needed; simply spray the rocks with water. Some people don't like the feel of walking on gravel because it can move around a lot under your feet. The other downside to gravel or stone is that wheelbarrows are impossible to use on it. If your greenhouse is big enough to use a wheelbarrow or dolly in, take this into consideration. Landscape rocks also work great; however, they are more expensive.

Pavers are generally used to create paths over dirt floors. This is necessary because the dirt floor will get muddy at times. They are also used to create solid walkways on gravel floors and as supports under tables and shelves.

If table legs are placed directly in the gravel, they can shift and sink over time. Pavers placed underneath them prevents this.

Placing a weed barrier cloth beneath the gravel or pavers is highly recommended. A weedmat can be bought at most garden supply stores. Cheap versions of weedmats aren't always effective and might still end up allowing weeds through, so make sure you get a well-reviewed one.

CONCRETE

A concrete floor provides a smooth, clean surface in your greenhouse. This flooring also retains heat during the day and naturally keeps your greenhouse warm. It is easy to move plants around and rearrange containers and growing trays. It is easy to wash and is nice to walk on. If you poured a concrete foundation, this also makes a great floor, which cuts down on building time and costs.

WOOD

Wooden floors are pretty; however, you will encounter the same problem with a wood floor that you would with a wood frame. Greenhouses are humid spaces, and wood floors can harbor diseases and mold. Also, they are likely to rot, even when you are using pressure treated wood meant for outdoors.

BRICK

Brick is an attractive choice for a greenhouse floor as well as being practical. Clay is porous and absorbs water which will provide additional humidity to your greenhouse. A layer of sand should be laid beneath the bricks for drainage and stability.

VINYL TILES

Gardening supply stores sell special vinyl tile that is made for greenhouses. It is porous, drains well, and is easy to clean. Vinyl tiles are comfortable to walk on and look nice. However, they are expensive compared to other flooring options.

MULCH

While mulch is easy to acquire, cheap, and simple to install as flooring, it is not recommended for greenhouse flooring. As it breaks down, it can introduce mold and insects into your greenhouse. Also, it is not a permanent flooring and will need to be replaced every year.

DIRT & GRAVEL COMBINATION

A popular method of greenhouse flooring is to install raised beds that keep the dirt floor underneath them with gravel or stone laid out everywhere else. This type of floor is ideal in many ways. The plants get the benefit of growing as deep as they need to into the dirt floor, and they also receive the warmth of the soil, which is particularly beneficial in colder months. The remainder of the greenhouse floor is cleaner and easier to walk on with gravel or stones as walkways. The downside to this configuration is that once you have built the raised beds, the design is permanent. Plants and beds can't be moved around at all, so if you choose this option, make sure you have it designed exactly how you want it.

FRAME

The type of material that is used for the frame will depend on where you are located and what type of greenhouse you want. Even if you are purchasing a greenhouse kit, it is important to pay attention to the type of frame material used. Aluminum, plastic, wood, and PVC are the most common choices.

ALUMINUM
Aluminum is great because it is inexpensive, doesn't rust and assembles easily. The not-so-great thing about aluminum is that it doesn't insulate, so that the greenhouse will lose heat through the frame. Aluminum can vary in strength and quality and not all aluminum frames can hold up against strong winds or heavy snow.

PLASTIC
Also inexpensive, plastic is a good choice for a frame. It doesn't have the insulation problem that aluminum does since it holds heat quite well. It is durable and weather resistant. The downside is that prolonged exposure to the sun can cause the plastic to expand and contract, leading it to warp. A light-colored plastic will limit this.

WOOD
Wood has been used for a long time to build greenhouses and is still a popular choice. It is

readily available, generally easy to work with, provides excellent strength, and is a good insulator. The thing to be wary of with wood is that because it is porous, it can be a haven for disease and mildew. Since greenhouses are damp, wet, spaces, this can be a real issue. A wooden greenhouse will need to be kept extra clean to prevent any outbreaks. The dampness in a greenhouse will likely cause the wood to rot as well, which means you will need to replace or rebuild it at some point. A high-quality, rot-resistant wood should be used such as cedar or redwood (also see information regarding pressure treated wood within the foundation section above).

PVC

The flexibility of PVC makes it a popular choice for hoop houses and tunnel greenhouses. It is simple to work with, lightweight, and inexpensive. It is also a great insulator. The downside to PVC is its lack of strength, which means it isn't great during strong winds or storms. The majority of greenhouses sold in kits use PVC frames.

GALVANIZED STEEL

Galvanized steel is another option that is popular in areas that have heavy snowfalls or strong winds. It is extremely strong and can hold up in many weather situations. The downsides are the weight, 3x that of aluminum, and the fact that the galvanizing will wear off over time and then it will rust. If you decide on galvanized pipe, use 1 1/2" pipe instead of 1" for extra strength. The 1" can still struggle to hold up under heavy snows. This is a good investment in climates where there is snow accumulation.

GLAZING

In greenhouse terminology, the type of covering around the greenhouse frame is called glazing. This is what lets the light and heat in from the sun. Traditionally, it has always been glass. In more recent times, plastic sheeting and polycarbonate have become popular as well.

GLASS

The traditional option, glass, is still a great choice. It lets in light easily, keeps the space warm and is generally easy to acquire. If properly cared for, a glass greenhouse can last decades. Single-pane glass is not a good insulator which can be a problem. A double or triple pane is better, yet of course it is more expensive, and glass is already the most expensive option.

The other problem with glass is that it breaks easily. Cleaning up shards of glass from your plants or soil is not good. It can also be difficult and time-consuming to replace because of its fragility.

PLASTIC (POLYETHYLENE) SHEETING

Plastic sheeting is great because it's inexpensive and easily available. It is the least expensive of all the options and does a good job of letting light in and holding in heat. If it gets ripped or punctured, it can be patched or replaced without too much difficulty. The biggest drawback with plastic is that it doesn't last forever. It will deteriorate from exposure to the elements and will need to be replaced every few years.

There is a type of plastic sheeting that is treated to resist ultraviolet rays. It is available at most greenhouse supply stores and is usually guaranteed for about four years. 6-mm plastic sheeting is recommended. Using two layers of this plastic as your glazing helps prolong its life a little more.

Regular utility grade plastic sheeting that is available everywhere is not recommended unless you want to replace it every year. It is the absolute cheapest and will do the job for one year. Once it starts to disintegrate though, it can become a real mess with little bits of plastic finding their way all over your greenhouse and garden. There are also other specially treated plastic sheeting options such as thermal protection, anti-condensation, and heat protection. For a greenhouse though, the UV rating is of the highest importance.

PLASTIC (POLYETHYLENE) PANELS

The same material used for plastic sheeting is also available in panels. The panels are usually double insulated, UV protected and good for about 10 years.

ACRYLIC

Also commonly known as plexiglass, acrylic is tough, durable, and slightly flexible. Acrylic panels can be complicated to install though because they expand and contract, so the attachments have to be very specific. It is also very expensive, about the same price as glass. Yet, it makes up for that by being extremely durable, lasting up to 20 years.

POLYCARBONATE TILES AND ROLLS

Polycarbonate is the newest glazing option to become available. It is amazing in all its properties. It lets light in better than glass or plastic, holds heat well and can be used on flat or curved surfaces. Polycarbonate is also lightweight and very strong. Panels are treated with a UV resistance to prevent yellowing and deterioration. It is less expensive than glass yet more expensive than plastic sheeting. Generally, it is guaranteed for about ten years.

SECURING AGAINST THE WIND

This is particularly important if your greenhouse is not on a permanent foundation. Cabled anchors are commonly used to secure a greenhouse. They include a set of four anchors, one for each corner, mounting hardware to secure it to the base, and cable to attach them. The anchors aren't too expensive, and if you live in a windy or stormy climate, it will be entirely worth it.

If you have a portable greenhouse, the edges can be weighed down with bricks, stone, or heavy wood pieces. A hoop house or tunnel greenhouse can be secured with tent pegs and rope. The frame poles should already be sunk at least 2' into the ground to prevent it from blowing over in the wind.

Hoop houses and tunnel greenhouses can also billow in the wind, like sails or giant kites. Fabric strapping zig-zagged across the roof will help keep the plastic in place and prevent it from flying away. Constructing your greenhouse in a sheltered location will also greatly reduce the chance of wind damage. Trees can provide shelter from wind, as can buildings and other structures. Building the greenhouse at a lower elevation than the land around you will also help protect it from the wind.

GREENHOUSE ENVIRONMENT

Keeping the environment in the greenhouse steady and controlled is important for the health and productivity of the plants. Greenhouses need to provide adequate temperature levels, sunlight, and humidity. The environment that you create in your greenhouse depends on what you are growing. Some plants need lots of heat while others thrive in cooler temperatures.

HEAT

Maintaining a steady temperature in a greenhouse can be quite difficult. During the day, the glazing materials let in heat and light with ease, causing the temperature to soar. Once night comes though, all the light is gone, and the heat dissipates quickly. It can swing from 100°F (38C) during the day to 30°F (-1C) at night (depending on where you live), which plants do not like. This type of fluctuation can hurt the productivity of the plants. Part of the purpose of heating is to stabilize the temperature within the greenhouse.

Tropical plants need temperatures above 70°F (21C) and high humidity. Cool-loving plants, like carrots, lettuce, radishes, peas, and beets, do well in greenhouses with a nighttime temperature of around 50°F (10C). Tomatoes and many flowering plants like nighttime temperatures to be around 65°F (18C). Research what temperature the plants you are growing will need, so you do not waste time and energy on heating if it isn't necessary. At the end of the book, you'll find an overview of the most common crops for the greenhouse and their temperature requirements. If you have a large greenhouse and only some of the plants need additional heat, arrange the plants together and set up the heating to concentrate on them. This will reduce your overall costs and allow you to grow a range of plants.

During cool and cold months, the temperature inside the greenhouse will fall at night. During the day, the sun will heat it enough to keep everything alive; however, once the sun is gone, so is the heat. If it is freezing outside, it will be freezing inside the greenhouse too, and your plants will not survive.

If your greenhouse is not insulated, any form of heating will be ineffective. Polycarbonate panels can keep heat in as well as double layered plastic sheeting. Of course, double layer plastic reduces light transmission, so there is a trade-off.

Heating a greenhouse can be expensive and possibly not worth the trouble or cost, depending on where and what you are planting. A goal of many home gardeners is to be sustainable, and spending a lot of money on heating is not viable. There are ways to keep heat in using minimalist methods that aren't expensive. They vary in effectiveness, and you will need to experiment a bit to see what works best for your arrangement.

Once you've decided on a type of heater, you'll need to figure out what size to get. One size definitely does not fit all since there are so many types and sizes of greenhouse. Determining what size heater to get takes a bit of math. First, you'll calculate the surface area of your greenhouse floor. Multiply the length of your greenhouse by the width to get this number. Once you know the surface area, you can seek out heating systems that cover it. Here is a greenhouse calculator you can use for your calculation: http://www.littlegreenhouse.com/heat-calc.shtml

There are several heating options available to help your plants make it through the cold temperatures.

PROPANE HEATER

These are generally inexpensive and are easy to set up. There are many options available to choose from. Most have several settings, so you can control how much heat is given off. There are some propane heaters designed specifically for greenhouses, but this type is of course more expensive. They are treated against rust, which is a real threat in a humid space such as a greenhouse.

ELECTRIC FAN HEATER (220-VOLT)

This, of course, requires that you have access to an electrical outlet. These heaters circulate air well and help prevent cold spots and disease development. If you go down this route, get a heater with a thermostat. This way, you can set it to only turn on when the temperature reaches a particular point. When the desired temperature is reached, the heater will automatically turn off. Having a system operate on its own reduces a lot of extra work and monitoring.

The placement of the fan heater within the greenhouse makes a big difference. Centrally located, open spots are best. One big benefit of this type of heater is that it can be moved around easily and then completely removed when it is no longer needed. This is great if space is a limited commodity in your greenhouse. Depending on the cost of electricity in your area, this can become expensive.

GAS OR OIL HEATERS

These are inexpensive options that provide decent heat. Open flame gas heaters should be avoided because they release ethylene gas which negatively affects growing plants. Ethylene gas doesn't have a smell, so it is near impossible to know there is a problem until it is too late. Plants will wilt, drop their flowers, and upper leaves will be twisted and deformed.

These types of heaters have oxygen safety sensors which will turn off the heater automatically when they sense there's not enough oxygen in the greenhouse. In a home, this is a good thing. In an air-tight greenhouse, it is not. Oxygen can be depleted easily in a well-insulated greenhouse. If the heater shuts off in the middle of the night because of this, it can cause the plants to die. A gas heater with an exhaust is best, and these require an outside vent for the exhaust to pass through.

SOLAR HEATERS

Installation of the solar panels and setting up the system will likely require a professional as it will need to be custom built. The panels have a food-grade antifreeze piped through them via a circulating pump. This system has given great results to gardeners who have it.

INEXPENSIVE OPTIONS

WOOD AND PELLET STOVES

Because fuel is expensive, wood is often a popular, cost-effective means of heating a greenhouse. They require proper set-up, circulation, and venting. If your greenhouse has plastic sheeting, a wood stove is not a good idea. Heat and plastic do not mix.

These types of stoves require tending and only provide heat for as long as you are feeding them. This is not a heat source that can be turned on and left alone. Depending on the size of the stove and your greenhouse, you may have to fill it with wood every few hours. Since most greenhouse set-ups need the heating at night, this means trips in the middle of the night.

There are mixed reports on the viability of pellet stoves. They work well, provide good heat, and are easy to maintain; however, they have been known to rust and stop working. The humidity in the greenhouse is its enemy.

RADIANT HEAT LAMPS

This type of heater looks like a lamp with a red light-bulb. It needs to be plugged in, so you will need access to an electrical outlet. It is hung over the plants, and its heat is sent directly downwards. They are inexpensive and come in a variety of sizes. Radiant heat lamps are best if there are only a few plants that need warming. They will not heat an entire greenhouse and don't distribute warmth anywhere but straight down.

FLOATING ROW COVER

While this isn't a heater, per se, it is a means of retaining heat in your greenhouse. Drape the row cover directly over the plants and it will keep the plants several degrees warmer than the room or the outside temperature. There are several types and weights to choose from, and the one you need will depend on the plants and the time of year. It is designed to allow light in while keeping insects and diseases out. It can be cut to size, and it is easy to move around to different areas of the garden. As the plants grow, they easily push the fabric up. Row cover is reusable and generally lasts one-two seasons. It can tear easily and deteriorate if not cared for properly.

FROST BLANKETS

Designed to protect seedlings, these are similar to row covers, yet are thicker and provide a lot more protection. They offer protection for plants down to 24°F (-4C). They can be used to extend the growing season in conjunction with a greenhouse or in place of a greenhouse.

CLOCHES

A cloche is another choice that is not a heater, yet will provide extra warmth to your plants. A cloche is a bell-shaped or square shaped container that is placed over the plants. Traditionally, they were made of glass, yet nowadays, they are often constructed of plastic. Most designs will provide a method of venting because it is easy for plants to overheat underneath them. They are designed to be placed over individual plants or a selection of plants.

ROCKS AND BRICKS

An inexpensive and easy way to add some heat to your greenhouse is to place rocks inside. During the day, they will collect the sun's heat and will release the heat at night and keep the space warm. Darker colored rocks will collect more heat. These should be placed near the plants for highest effectiveness.

BUBBLE WRAP

This is an insulator rather than a heater. If you are looking for a low budget option to retain heat in your greenhouse, this is a good choice. Secure a layer of bubble wrap on the inside walls of the greenhouse to reduce heat loss and block draughts. Horticulture bubble wrap insulation is made specifically for this purpose and can be found at a garden supply store. It is UV treated and toughened for use.

Having an additional layer of plastic in your greenhouse will reduce the amount of light that comes in by approximately 10%. This will negatively impact the growth of your plants. Choose a bubble wrap with larger sized bubbles as this will let in more light. This only helps a little though.

Bubble wrap can be used to provide a partition between areas of your greenhouse. With partitions, you can use a heater in sections just for certain plants. This reduces wasted energy and the wasted cost of heating an entire greenhouse when you only need a small portion heated.

It is important to remember, regardless of which heater you choose, to make sure your greenhouse is vented. Also, the heating system should have an automatic shut-off.

HEATED PROPAGATOR MAT

These are mats that can be purchased at gardening supply stores. They are set underneath pots and trays of seedlings and send heat upwards. They are electrical and need to be plugged in.

SHADE

The amount of shade a greenhouse gets is important. This may seem odd since greenhouses are designed to bring in the maximum amount of light and heat from the sun, and those that bring in the most are considered better. However, greenhouses are about microclimates and management. Sun is great. Too much sun is not great. And it will vary at different times of the year. Remember, as seasons change, so do the hours of sunlight, and this has a direct effect on the health of your plants.

Plants can be burned in the summer months when they are receiving long hours of direct light. The leaves will be discolored and look bleached. To protect them, it is necessary to provide shading of some sort. There are a variety of options such as vinyl plastic shading, roll up screens, polypropylene shade cloth, and paint on materials.

Shading is complicated by the fact that plants need light and any shade limits that. It is about finding a good balance. It is better to err on the side of caution and provide the minimal amount of shade needed. The temperature inside your greenhouse should not exceed 81°F (27C).

EXTERNAL BLINDS

External blinds attach to the outside of your greenhouse. They provide excellent shade since they block the sun before it hits your windows. They are easy to use and are easily manipulated. Putting them all the way down or partially down is not a problem, and you can set them how you like. The biggest downside to this type of shade is their cost. They are on the expensive side. Additionally, depending on your greenhouse setup, they may interfere with the operation of your vents. External blinds can be set up on a remote.

INTERNAL BLINDS

Internal blinds are not as effective as external blinds because they block the sun after it has already passed through the windows. They do work well though and are popular as a shade. Like external blinds, they are easily adjusted and can be lowered all the way or partially. And each blind can be set to a different height which gives the gardener a large amount of control. Some internal blind systems can also be controlled via remote.

SHADE CLOTH/NETTING

The material used for shade cloth can vary; however, the most important thing to pay attention to with shade cloth is its filtration rating. They are usually listed as 40%, 50%, 60%, or 70% and refer to how much sunlight they will block. Which one you need depends on your particular situation. In most cases, 40%-50% is sufficient unless the greenhouse is south-facing and gets non-stop sun all day long.

Shade cloth can be hung on the interior or exterior of the greenhouse. Hanging the cloth on the outside will be more effective since it will block the sun before it hits the glazing. For some people, the aesthetics of an external shade are undesirable. An external shade cloth will also degrade quicker than an internal one since it is more exposed to the elements.

A common shade cloth material is aluminized polyester. This reflects light instead of just blocking it, making it extremely effective. Aluminum curtains can also be used at night to keep heat in.

Another popular choice is polyethylene plastic because it is inexpensive. It is usually knitted or knotted together in some fashion to form a type of cloth or cohesive material. It is UV treated to withstand the sun.

Shade cloth is attached with hooks, clips, or grommets. Manufactured options will have the attachment kit included.

This option is less expensive than blinds, however it will degrade quicker (both internal and external) and will need to be replaced more often.

SHADE PAINT

Applied externally to the glass, these paints work quite well. There are several brands on the market to choose from. Several layers of paint can be added, depending on the needs of the season. When you don't need it anymore, it washes off. These paints are not recommended for acrylic or polycarbonate windows as they don't wash off well. Shade paints are not expensive. The main difficulty in using them is that it is hard to apply a uniform coating.

DIY SHADE CLOTH

Home gardeners have reported success using burlap cloth, and even plain white bed sheets as shade cloth. In a pinch, either of these will work well. For a long-term solution though, it is recommended to get something specifically made for shading greenhouses.

NATURAL SHADE

Trees, buildings, and structures can provide natural cooling for your greenhouse. The shadow from these objects is shading that can be counted on every day. Sometimes, it is problematic since it can't generally be moved; however, if you work the natural shade into your greenhouse plan, you can really make it work for you.

VENTILATION/ COOLING

When the greenhouse is receiving lots of direct sun for long hours, it is possible for the plants to become overheated. This is different from burning. Overheating will cause the plants to wilt and die. Proper ventilation is also required to prevent the spread of diseases in the humid environment. Having a source of ventilation that can be manipulated as needed is extremely important. In a greenhouse, there are three main places that air can come in and out. The first is the main door. It can be opened or closed as needed throughout the day to provide air flow. The second is roof vents, and the third is side vents.

Most greenhouses have hand-operated vents or flaps that can be opened and closed when necessary. There are also electric and temperature sensitive vent options available. An oscillating fan will provide good air flow. Some greenhouse designs, like the hoop house, can have roll-up sides which is great for ventilation. The majority of greenhouse kits will have roof and side vents already installed.

Smaller greenhouses generally have a greater ventilation need since they have a higher glass to floor ratio. There is less space for heat to spread out, and it is being heated at a fast rate, so if you purchase or build a small greenhouse, monitor the heat carefully.

To properly understand the ventilation needs of your greenhouse, a thermostat should be installed inside. A remote access one is especially handy. The temperature inside should not exceed 81° F (27C) as temperatures higher than that can cause problems with your plants.

There is no cookie cutter method to ventilating a greenhouse. As with so many things, it depends on a lot of different factors. For example, the size and type of greenhouse, whether there is access to electricity, what you're growing, and the gardener's budget. In general though, an automatic system is greatly preferred over a manual one. Having vents that open automatically makes a big difference to the welfare of your plants and your workload.

Keep an eye on the health of your plants by checking for leaf scorching, wilting, and extreme dryness. These are signs that you need more ventilation or that your current system is not working.

PASSIVE AND POWERED VENTILATION SYSTEMS

There are two types of ventilation systems: passive and powered. Passive ventilation systems have no mechanical parts. The most basic vents are passive. These are great in terms of simplicity, ease of use, and if noise is an issue. A passive (also called natural) ventilation system depends on thermal buoyancy for air movement. When air is heated, it rises naturally, and as the air rises, it flows out of the roof vents. Vents installed on the side walls suck in fresh air as the hot air leaves. This ensures there is always good air circulation around the plants.

A passive system is still at the mercy of the

outside temperatures. It can keep the air flowing and keep the inside temperature lower by degrees; however, it won't maintain a consistent temperature.

A passive system is not as effective as a powered one, yet it is more cost-effective than a powered system since it doesn't require electricity. It is a great choice for any greenhouse and is ideal if your greenhouse is located somewhere without access to electricity.

Powered ventilation systems incorporate fans and often temperature-controlled thermostats, so the system can turn on and off on its own. This type of system is more accurate than a passive system, and it is easier to keep the greenhouse at a specific temperature. The increase in temperature control is a huge bonus, especially if you are growing highly temperature sensitive plants. Additionally, powered ventilation systems provide a closed system in your greenhouse which means pests and debris can't get in through open vents. They are, of course, much more expensive. Fans used in a powered system can cause quite a bit of noise. If your greenhouse is attached to the side of your house, keep this in mind when deciding which system to use. The noise levels may be disturbing.

DOORS

Propped open doors are a simple, effective way to bring fresh air into a greenhouse. Every greenhouse has a door, so this is an easy option. It won't provide adequate ventilation since the air is only coming from one direction, yet it is a start. Depending on the size and layout of your greenhouse, it may only make a dent in the air flow that the plants need. However, since it's such an easy thing to do, it shouldn't be overlooked. If your greenhouse has two doors, that is much better. Propping them both open will create a good cross-breeze.

HAND OPERATED VENTS

Simply put, this type of vent is either on your wall or the roof and operates with a hand crank. These vents are easy to use, don't require any special tools, electricity, or know-how. There is no equipment that can break down which makes them ideal for a simple, no-frills, greenhouse design. Most prefabricated greenhouses come with a hand crank vent.

The biggest downside to this type of ventilation, and it can be a huge hurdle for many gardeners, is that you must be there to operate it. This can require extra planning every day to ensure that the vents are opened and closed at the necessary times. If you work outside the home and aren't there to vent the greenhouse during the hottest parts of the day, it can be fatal for your plants. Particularly during the summer months, the weather will need to be checked every morning before leaving the house, and the greenhouse vented in anticipation of mid-day temperatures. It is an extra chore and is a big problem if it is forgotten.

ELECTRIC VENTS
These vents are the same as hand operated vents in style and size. The difference is that the vents are not opened manually. Some are attached to a control system, so you only have to press a button for them to open. This can be helpful since it will reduce the effort needed to open the vents. In a large greenhouse, this can be a key issue, especially if the vents need to be opened and closed often. Alternately, the vents can be connected to a thermostat, so that they will open and close automatically depending on the temperature inside the greenhouse.

TEMPERATURE SENSITIVE/AUTOMATIC VENTS
These vents are really neat and a great way to provide circulation in your greenhouse. They work via solar power and don't require any electricity. The cylinder mechanism of these vents operates through heat build-up in the greenhouse. As heat builds, the vents slowly open. When it gets cooler, the vents slowly close. It is entirely automatic, and once it's set up, requires virtually no care. They are very easy to set up. The cylinders do wear out after a while but they are easy to replace.

This type of vent operates solely on the temperature inside the greenhouse. They will not close if it starts to rain unless the rain brings a drop in temperature.

EXHAUST FAN
An exhaust fan will move and refresh the stale air in the greenhouse. They are usually mounted on the roof and draw the hot air up and send it outside. Exhaust fans can be motorized or non-motorized. The motorized ones are, of course, more expensive. They provide more air flow than vents, and therefore make it easier to maintain a specific temperature inside the greenhouse.

OSCILLATING FANS
Oscillating fans are a quick, simple tool to bring air movement into the greenhouse. They are inexpensive and are extremely handy since they are portable and so can be moved around the greenhouse as needed. Having

several of these on hand to focus on specific areas or plants can make a big difference.

ROLL UP SIDES (HOOP HOUSES AND TUNNEL GREENHOUSES)
Hoop houses and tunnel greenhouses can be simple to ventilate since the sides of the structure can be designed to roll up as needed. Some systems require manual lifting of the sides and others have automatic controls. The entire side of the hoop house can be set to roll up or just a portion of the side. Fresh air rushes in and pushes the warm air out, creating a good flow of air around the plants. The electricity costs of this type of set up are significantly less than using fans. It can be combined with a thermostat to operate automatically, raising and lowering to maintain a prespecified temperature.

EVAPORATIVE COOLING MATS
These mats are available at gardening stores. They use the hot air in the greenhouse to evaporate water from the plants and other wet surfaces to bring the temperature down. They can bring the temperature down 10-20° F (-12 to -7C) below the outside temperature. These mats generally work best in dry climates, yet can be effective anywhere.

The mats are mounted on the wall of the greenhouse and supplied with water to keep them wet. The pads need to be continuously wet in order to work properly. Hot outside air flows through them, creating the cooling effect, or a fan can be mounted on the opposite wall to create air flow.

Cooling mats are an easy system to use once installed. They do the job automatically, so you don't have to worry about cooling. They don't need electricity or batteries.

WIRELESS SYSTEMS
Wireless systems provide a lot of new and exciting possibilities, taking garden automation to the next level. Ventilation of the greenhouse can be monitored from a computer or cell phone, possibly through an app. These systems usually gather data as they operate which can be reviewed for possibilities of greater efficiency. Also, if there is a problem, it will be discovered sooner.

HUMIDITY

Measuring and monitoring the humidity in your greenhouse is extremely important for the health of your plants. Relative humidity is a measure of the amount of water in the air. The problem with excess humidity is that it causes the leaves on your plants to get wet. Leaves that are wet for an extended period of time are prime locations for a disease to bloom. The diseases are then easily spread when moisture, caused by the humidity, builds up on the roof and drips down onto all the plants. An outbreak can happen very quickly.

Relative humidity is measured by how much moisture the air can hold. Warmer temperatures hold more moisture. A greenhouse with a temperature of 70°F will hold up to five times more moisture than the same air at 30°F. Water drops condense on cars, grass, and plants when the air reaches its saturation point, called the dew point. A psychrometer measures the humidity in the air and is a good tool to have on hand.

In a greenhouse, moisture comes from several places. It evaporates up from the soil; plants give moisture off naturally, and, of course, it comes from watering the plants.

To combat moisture, the best thing is to make sure the air inside the greenhouse is always circulating. Ventilating it will make a huge difference (see above section on ventilation). Appropriate plant spacing and watering will help a lot too and so will well-drained floors. Keeping the greenhouse dry will also have a big impact. This is especially important when the temperature drops as if there are puddles, they will evaporate and cause moisture build-up in the air.

It is good practice to water the plants only as much as they need, so there is no excess water pooling in the greenhouse. Watering in the morning gives the plant surfaces time to dry before the temperature drops in the evening.

The leaf canopy of your plants is where the

highest relative humidity can be found. This is caused by transpiration. Transpiration is the passage of water through a plant and its evaporation through the plant's leaves, stems, and flowers. Plants adapt the amount of water they take in through their roots based on the surrounding temperature. If plants are spaced too closely together, or there isn't adequate air circulation, the moisture gets trapped in the leaf canopy. Weeds are also a big contributor to transpiration.

On hot days, plants will take in more water to keep themselves cool. When the temperature lowers at night, they slow the water intake naturally. If there are sudden increases or decreases in temperature, which, in turn, affects the humidity, the plants can't react fast enough and will show signs of stress. The damage to the plants can be reduced or eliminated if the plants have enough time to adjust. Take measures to reduce humidity in stages, so they have this time.

LIGHTING

The majority of light in your greenhouse will be provided naturally by the sun. During extended periods of sunless days and during the winter, you may need to supplement the amount of light your plants are getting. Plants need a minimum of six hours of light with some varieties needing a lot more to thrive. Do not give your plants more than twelve hours of light. They need downtime, and too much light will cause them to grow oddly. Younger plants, in general, need less light than older plants. The greatest need for light when they are older is to facilitate blooming. Group plants with similar light requirements in the same area. This will make it easier to provide each plant type with the correct amount of light. You can find details on lighting requirements for each plant at the end of this book.

The lighting that you need for your greenhouse will depend on the available hours of sunlight, what time of year it is, what plants you are growing, and how much you want to spend. Many greenhouse growers install a combination of different lights for maximum benefits.

COMPACT FLUORESCENT BULBS (CFLS)

An inexpensive and effective choice is compact fluorescent light bulbs. They are a type of light bulb that can screw directly into an existing light socket. This makes them easy to set up because they don't need special wiring. CFLs provide full-spectrum lighting, which is the same as that emitted by the sun. These light bulbs are ideal because they are similar to sunlight, and also shine the light in all directions, which is great for greenhouses. The packaging for the light bulbs will indicate the temperature range. When your plants are young, they will do well with a lower temperature rating, and when they mature, they will benefit from a higher temperature rating. And, because they are light bulbs, all you need to do is switch them out which makes things very easy.

T-5 FLUORESCENT LIGHTS

These come in four-foot lengths and are installed in the ceiling above your plants. They are cost-effective, powerful, and efficient lights. Horticulture bulbs are available and come in red or blue. And, the T-5 light fixtures can often hold multiple bulbs which means you can customize the lights for your greenhouse.

The standard fluorescent light, the T-12, can be used, however it does not have the same intensity and efficiency as T-5s.

METAL HALIDE

This type of light has a high-intensity discharge (HID) and is more intense than fluorescent lighting. They provide the blue light spectrum that plants need for vegetative growth. The lights come in 400, 600, and 1000 watts. They produce lots of heat and consist of a bulb, ballast, and socket base. These lights work well, however they require a lot of electricity, making them a non-economical choice for many gardeners.

HIGH-PRESSURE SODIUM (HPS) LAMPS

Another type of HID light, the HPS lamps provide light on the red spectrum, as opposed to blue like the metal halide ones. The red spectrum is good for flowering and fruiting plants. They come in 400, 600, and 1000 watts. The set up for these lamps requires a bulb, ballast, and socket base.

METAL HALIDE AND HPS COMBINATION

Purchasing a convertible ballast will allow you to use both a metal halide and HPS bulb in the same socket. Not at the same time though. The metal halide can be used while the plant is young and growing, and then it can be switched out for the HPS for the flowering stage.

LIGHT EMITTING DIODE (LED) LIGHT

LED lights are extremely energy efficient which is quickly making them a top choice among greenhouse growers. Energy costs can add up fast if there is a need to have the lights on a frequently. These lights are expensive; however, their long life makes up for it. They can last 8-10 years. Another benefit is that LED lights don't get nearly as hot to touch as regular light bulbs. This means they can be placed close to the plants without as much worry about the temperature. There are LED lights designed specifically for growing plants, and they have adjustable red, white, and blue lights. For those that need precision, these are the best choice.

IRRIGATION

Setting up a watering system in your greenhouse will significantly cut down on the work needed to maintain it. There are three basic rules about watering. First, the planting medium should drain well. A plant cannot be watered well if the medium does not drain properly. Second, watering needs to be thorough every time. The water needs to reach the roots for a healthy plant to grow. Check this by moving the soil aside a few inches deep with your finger. If it is still dry an inch down, the plant needs more water. Third, water before the plant gets stressed out. This often means the soil will be dry but not parched. An irrigation system can ensure that the plants are getting all the water they need and at the appropriate times.

HAND WATERING

Simple and self-explanatory, hand watering is holding the hose or can in your hand to apply water to the plants. This is, of course, the most time intensive and inefficient method. It is also the least expensive and easiest to do.

MISTING SYSTEM

A mister sends water droplets over the tops of the plants. The system is attached to the roof of the greenhouse. Misting systems can be set up to deliver water to the plants on a schedule for the highest effectiveness. These are most often used in greenhouses that contain all the same kind of plant and therefore need all the same regime of watering.

Nozzles can become clogged, so the system needs to be checked regularly and maintained consistently. Another downside is that a lot of water is wasted since the mist goes everywhere. Water can pool up on floors and elsewhere.

DRIP TUBES

Drip tubes are specially made hoses that have many tiny holes in them. The system is set up with a pump and sends small amounts of water out at a time. The system supports multiple tubes which extend out from the main water supply. The tubes can be buried into the soil around the plant or placed on the soil around them. The system can be set up manually, or automatically with timers and motion sensors.

These are better than the misting system because they don't get the plants' leaves wet. Over-wet leaves can encourage mold and disease.

MAT IRRIGATION

Specialty mats are placed under the container holding the plant. The mats are kept constantly moist through a drip line system. Plants wick up water from the mats as needed, creating a self-watering system. There is no worry of over-watering or under-watering with this system.

GREENHOUSE EQUIPMENT

THERMOMETER
Temperature is of utmost importance when managing a greenhouse. Thermometers range in cost from simple and inexpensive to ultra-fancy and very expensive. A high/low thermometer will display the highest temperature during the day and lowest at night. This is extremely useful when planning your heating and cooling requirements.

POTTING CONTAINERS
Pots in a variety of sizes will be necessary to grow plants. What size you specifically need will depend on what you are growing. Having specific seed starter flats is extremely helpful for starting any seeds.

GARDENING TOOLS
The basics, a trowel, shovel, rake, hand fork, pruners, and a watering can. If there is space, a wheelbarrow will be very useful. Designate an area of your greenhouse for tool storage. It is amazing how quickly things can go missing or get misplaced. A marker and labels are also good to have on hand if you are growing a variety of plants.

SINK OR WASHTUB
Having a place to rinse garden tools, wash vegetables, and clean pots is very handy.

CLEANING SUPPLIES
Insecticidal spray, disinfectant spray, and bleach are a few good things to have in the greenhouse to keep everything clean and free of pests and disease.

BENCH AND/OR SHELVES
A staging area to do your gardening work is very helpful. When you are transplanting or starting seeds, you always need space on which to set pots, flats, and soil.

Benches and shelves are also needed to hold the pots. Keeping them on the floor is not a good idea for the plant's health.

HUMIDITY MONITOR/PSYCHROMETER
Since humidity can be so tricky in a greenhouse, having a tool that monitors it is invaluable. There are handheld as well as permanently installed versions.

SOIL TEMPERATURE THERMOMETER
Throughout this guide, there are many mentions of soil temperature. Proper soil temperature is critical for seed germination and thriving plant growth. Soil temperatures inside a greenhouse can vary, too.
The temperature of the ground soil will not be the same as the soil in raised beds or planters. Using a soil thermometer removes any guesswork and ensures you plant at the right time. There are analog and digital soil thermometers, and both work great.

Chapter 3

GROWING IN YOUR GREENHOUSE

SEEDS, PLANTING, POLLINATION

Once you have chosen your greenhouse, built it, and set it up, it is time for the real fun to begin. Growing plants in a greenhouse environment is different from growing them outside in a garden or inside in a grow room. Some things are similar, however there are a variety of different things to consider.

This section will walk you through the process of growing plants from start to finish, including detailed explanations for growing specific vegetables, fruits, and herbs.

STARTING SEEDS

A greenhouse is not always an ideal place to start plants from seed. It can get too hot during the day unless there is careful temperature control and lots of ventilation. During cold months, the temperature can be too low for the delicate seeds to germinate.

To start seedlings in a greenhouse, be sure to monitor the temperature and keep in mind that different types of plants like different temperatures. A greenhouse that is set up with a lighting and venting system will be much better for starting seeds than one without.

Alternately, seeds grown in winter will have the opposite problem. During the day, the seeds are warm and happy. Once night falls and the temperature drops, the germination process can be terminated, and the seeds will be lost. The temperature should be at least 50°F (10C) at all times, with the optimal temperature being between 65°F-80°F (18-27C). If you are starting seeds in winter in your greenhouse, you will need an additional heat source. Please see the section about planting in winter for more information about this.

Starting seeds in a greenhouse is a great way to jump-start the growing season and have seedlings ready to plant in the ground as soon as the outside temperature allows. If this is your goal, start your seedlings in the greenhouse 6-8 weeks before the last frost date for your area. If it is too cold at night for the seedlings, you can use heat mats under them. Seedling heat mats can alleviate the issue of low temperatures. They require electricity which means your greenhouse will need access to power to take advantage of this. Starting seeds in a cold frame greenhouse without an additional heat source is not viable until the outside temperatures are amenable.

There are cool weather plants (kale, cabbage, broccoli) and hot weather plants (tomatoes, peppers, eggplant), and if the temperature is an issue, you can choose ones that are better suited for your greenhouse. Read the seed packets to see which ones will work best for your situation.

PLANTING

Seeds can be planted in open flat seed trays or in individual plug trays. There are several different options on the market that work well. Reusable Styrofoam plug trays are a good choice and come in a variety of plug sizes. The benefit of individual plug trays over flat seed trays is that with the individual ones, the roots of the plants don't intertwine, which can make them difficult to remove. Also, the seedlings can be popped out easily and placed in the garden.

A general all-purpose potting mix will work well. Many people prefer a soil-less mix. Plant the seeds according to the depth indicated on the packet. It varies by seed. Often, seeds are planted too deeply when all they need is a light covering. Planting them too deeply means they will likely not germinate. The trays should be on tables or benches to germinate.

If your greenhouse has dirt floors and that is the only place you intend to plant seeds, you will have to wait until the soil is warm enough to get started. This will be sooner than if you were planting in the soil outside since the sun is heating the inside soil like a battery.

WATERING

In the beginning, seedlings only need a light mist of water. They can drown or rot if they are over-watered, so go easy. Of course, they can also die if they aren't watered enough. A good rule of thumb is to mist them until the soil is moist, and that's it. They need to be watered at least twice a day to prevent them from drying out. A spray bottle is a good way to water newly planted seeds. When the seeds have germinated, they can be watered deeper, and it is good to allow the soil to dry between watering.

LIGHT
Newly planted seeds need between 14-16 hours of light. Using grow lights may be necessary depending on where you live and what time of year it is. The lights should be adjustable, so you can raise them higher as the plants grow. In the beginning, you want them to be as close to the seedlings as possible without touching them.

POLLINATION
Plant pollination happens in nature through birds, bees, butterflies, and the wind. A greenhouse, with its controlled environment, is a barrier to all these. This means alternate methods of pollination must happen for your plants to produce fruits. Manual pollination is done by gently shaking or tapping flowers to release the pollen. Different plants have different ways of pollinating. For example, a squash is either male or female. The pollen needs to be transferred from one plant to the other. Each tomato plant has both male and female flowers, so the pollen needs to be disturbed enough so it distributes within itself.

Garden and greenhouse supply companies sell battery operated pollinating devices. They are handheld wands that vibrate the flower head gently. A hand-held electric toothbrush will serve the same purpose. For best results, pollinate plants every day in the morning.

GREENHOUSE GROWING OPTIONS

A greenhouse provides a space where you can grow vegetables in several different ways. Raised beds, containers, and direct soil planting all have their own unique benefits and downsides. Most greenhouse growers use a combination of all these methods to get the most out of their greenhouse space.

RAISED BEDS

The pros to a raised bed are more control of soil quality, temperature fluctuations, and accessibility. If you have space for even one raised bed, it will significantly enhance your greenhouse gardening experience. Raised beds need to be filled with potting soil mix, which can get expensive, and that is a considerable downside. A raised bed is easier to work around and is ideal for anyone with mobility challenges. They're easy to monitor and harvest from and are a key to successful root vegetable growing.

Since raised beds are above ground level and enclosed, they naturally retain more heat in winter. Greenhouse growers in northern climates will benefit greatly from this when overwintering crops.

Most vegetables can grow in a raised bed, but you must consider the entire life of the vegetable and how the temperatures in the greenhouse will change over the months. For example, beets like cool weather and will bolt in the heat. They may be fine started in the greenhouse in May or June, but in a month or two will be struggling in the hot greenhouse.

POTTING CONTAINERS

Like raised beds, potting containers and grow bags provide a more valuable service to growers. They insulate the potting soil and seeds more, making them a good choice for temperature-sensitive vegetables. Black grow bags, in particular, retain warmth significantly more than either soil planting or other containers.

Potting containers, like raised beds, need potting soil, which can become pricey. The most significant upside to pots, containers, and grow bags is that they're movable. For gardeners with limited greenhouse space, this is a game-changer. The pots can be moved in and out of the greenhouse as needed and grow bags can be folded up and packed away when not in use.

Potting containers are an excellent option if you intend to grow any root vegetables to maturity in the greenhouse. They're also great for planting tomatoes, peppers, and other space-hungry plants that can then be moved around as they grow.

In cooler climates, when the winter is turning to spring, you can move potted plants outdoors to enjoy the warm sun, then bring them back into the greenhouse to protect them from nighttime chills. The reverse is also possible; when the weather transitions from fall to winter, potted plants brought into the greenhouse will produce longer.

DIRECT SEEDING

You can plant directly in the soil if you've got a dirt floor in your greenhouse. This is a great way to employ otherwise overlooked space; for example, lettuce easily fits in unused nooks and crannies.

Direct seeding is beneficial because it doesn't require the purchase of potting soil. However, direct-seeded plants can't be moved if they get big, are struggling, or temperatures are too extreme in a particular position.

If planted at the proper times, carrots, beets, lettuce, and Asian greens will thrive when direct-seeded. Depending on your growing season, short-season warm-weather crops such as cucumbers, beans, and herbs can also be direct seeded. These will do well planted in late spring and then watered well when the temperatures rise. Longer season tomatoes, peppers, and eggplant possibly won't have enough time to reach maturity when direct-seeded. Again, this depends on where you live.

SEED STARTING & TRANSPLANTING

Many people use their greenhouse solely for starting seeds to be transplanted to the garden. Greenhouses provide the ideal location to start seeds since they're protected and can be moderately temperature regulated. Seed starting, though, takes a lot of space. This must be considered if you're using the greenhouse space to grow mature plants. Shelving helps a lot and is a necessity for more extensive gardens.

Seed starting doesn't just have to be done for transplanting to the garden. Starting seeds early in the greenhouse also quickens the growth of greenhouse-only plants.

OPTIONS

- Start seeds in the greenhouse, transplant them to the garden
- Start seeds in the greenhouse, transplant them to raised beds or containers in the greenhouse
- Start seeds in the greenhouse, transplant to the greenhouse soil floor
- Due to residual solar heat, an unheated greenhouse is generally 5-10 degrees Fahrenheit (3-6 degrees Celsius) warmer than outdoor temperatures.

WHAT TO EXPECT

- During the winter months, plants will grow slowly or not at all, but that doesn't mean they're dead; they're just resting. In spring, many of them will rejuvenate.

- You can still harvest in the winter from the slow-growing plants; just know it is limited. If you want large winter harvests, you'll need to plan that out in advance. Winter gardening starts in August and September; plant enough then to tide you over through the colder months.

- Winter-grown plants may not reach full maturity. That's okay; harvest what you have. For example, beets may not grow large bulbs in winter, but small bulbs and beet greens are harvestable and delicious.

- In cold climates, overwintered plants will need mulching, row covers, and fabric hoop frames to protect them. The plants will freeze and die without this.

- During winter, the greenhouse soil is warmer than the air. This gives root vegetables insulation and often allows them to grow throughout the winter.

- Always be realistic. You're not going to grow tomatoes in an unheated greenhouse in January in a cold climate.

LOCATION AND CLIMATE CONSIDERATIONS

The greenhouse calendar will not be the same for every climate zone. A greenhouse in a warm southern location will operate on a slightly different schedule than one in a 4-season climate. However, this calendar can be adapted to any environment; you just may need to alter the starting month.

CLIMATE

Do you live in a cold, northern location with minimal sunlight during the winter months, or do you live in a warm, southern area where the temperatures reach unbearable heights in summer? These factors will influence how you plan your greenhouse.

In a southern location, greenhouse growing in the summer is impossible unless you have shade cloth, venting, fans, and a watering system. The plants will quickly overheat without these additions. Daily monitoring of daytime temperatures is essential during the summer months in southern climates.

On the other hand, in a cool northern location, plants will struggle in the coldest parts of winter without extra heating and light. These considerations are unique to your specific situation. Make sure you understand your climate thoroughly before growing anything.

LAYERS OF PROTECTION

You can "adjust" your grow zone through shade cloths or row covers. The general rule is that every layer of protection adds (or subtracts) 1.5 zones to your standard zone. The greenhouse itself is one layer – the windows being a layer of protection from the outdoor climate.

If you use row covers on your crops in winter, that counts as two layers – the greenhouse windows and the row cover. Covering the greenhouse with a shade cloth equals two layers – the greenhouse windows plus the shade cloth.

Example: A zone 5 hardiness (according to the USDA hardiness zone map) unheated greenhouse employing a row cover is providing two layers of protection. Each layer adds a 1.5 zone adjustment. This makes the zone 5 greenhouse act more like a zone 8 greenhouse.

THE MATH
2 LAYERS X **1.5** ZONE INCREASE PER LAYER = **3**

USDA Hardiness Zone Map

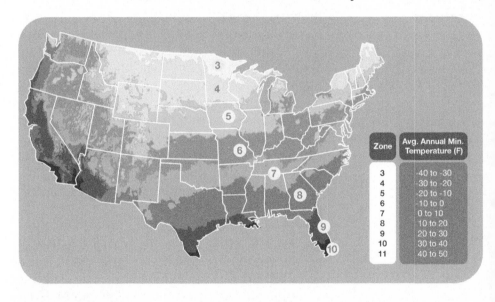

Zone	Avg. Annual Min. Temperature (F)
3	-40 to -30
4	-30 to -20
5	-20 to -10
6	-10 to 0
7	0 to 10
8	10 to 20
9	20 to 30
10	30 to 40
11	40 to 50

DAY LENGTH

This zone increase is still seasonal though. In the above scenario, the unheated greenhouse is now rated a zone 8, but that is only for zone 8 winter crops. You cannot grow zone 8 summer crops in the greenhouse in winter.

One of the most important considerations when growing in a greenhouse is day-length. Day-length determines how much light and heat your greenhouse receives. These will both have a considerable impact on the success of your crops, especially seedling starts.

Seedlings generally won't grow if they don't receive at least 10-12 hours of light per day. In northern climates, this isn't possible without supplemental lighting and heat sources. It isn't just that the daylight hours aren't long enough; there are also many cloudy, overcast, or snowy days where there is minimal sunlight even during the peak of the day.

Before you start planning your greenhouse, figure out the average day lengths for your area so you can plan appropriately.

Example: In zone 5, daylight hours drop below 10 in November. Then, it isn't until February that the days begin lengthening to 10 hours again. So, growing in the greenhouse between November and February means insufficient daylight and heat. Some plants will still grow during this time if they are planted early enough, and plants that have reached maturity before November can be harvested throughout the winter.

Folks in this climate zone will need to plan carefully for those months if they want to have fresh vegetables. Or they will need to set up lighting and heating in the greenhouse so plants will grow and new seedlings can be started.

TEMPERATURE

Most greenhouses have micro-climates inside – areas where it is colder or warmer than the rest of the greenhouse. It is crucial to know where these are located so you don't plant cold-tender plants in a particularly drafty area. Temperatures will change through the seasons – the greenhouse location, construction, type, and orientation play a prominent role in this.

The side that gets the most sun will be significantly warmer than the opposite end of the greenhouse. The coldest areas are usually by vents and any doors or windows. This is the best place for cold-hardy vegetables, such as kale and spinach. The north wall will be the warmest, where the sun reflects off the panes.

Plan the planting schedule for your greenhouse with climate, day length, and plant location in mind, and you'll be able to harvest successfully year-round.

CHALLENGES OF GREENHOUSE GARDENING

1. The biggest issue is always temperature regulation. Even in the depths of winter, a greenhouse can get too hot during the day and plants may wilt. Then, at night, it's back to freezing temperatures. Proper ventilation is essential, as well as careful monitoring of daytime and nighttime temperatures. It's important to be flexible. A ventilation system connected to a thermostat makes a huge difference.

2. In the winter, vegetables might freeze. However, this isn't problematic for many winter vegetables. Carrots and beets taste better after a couple of freezes. Lettuce, on the other hand, likely won't recover.

HOW TO PLAN YOUR GREENHOUSE GROWING CALENDAR

What you'll need:

- Paper or digital 12-month calendar that you can write or type on.

- Pen

- A couple of hours

1. Look up the average first and last frost dates for your area. Mark them on the calendar.

2. Look up day lengths for your area – when does day-length drop below 10 hours of sunlight in winter? And, when does day-length increase again to more than 10 hours of sunlight per day? Mark these dates on your calendar.

3. Write down the average temperature highs and lows for day and night for each month.

4. Make a list of all the vegetables you want to grow.

5. Plan the winter garden first – look at each vegetable you want to plant and time it so they will mature before the daylight hours fall below 10 per day or the ground freezes. Pay attention to germination temperatures and consider that lower fall temperatures will cause vegetables to mature slower.

6. Now, take all the other veggies you want to plant and consult the month-by-month chart to see how early they can be started. Take into consideration whether you're growing in the ground, raised beds, or containers, as well as what types of layering or shading you'll be using for extra protection during the hottest and coldest months.

7. Write down the start date for each vegetable. Include successive plantings, where applicable, and don't forget the practical considerations such as space availability and your own time/energy constraints.

8. As you're writing out your planting calendar, consult the day-lengths and monthly temperature highs and lows that you've already written down to ensure it will work out.

EXAMPLE

New York City is in zone 7 hardiness (according to the USDA hardiness zone map). The average last frost is April 5th, and the average first frost is November 12th. This equates to 220 days in the normal growing season. The day-length drops below 10 hours in mid-November, then in late-January, goes back to above 10 hours.

A person in this location will write all this information down on their monthly calendar. Then, take a look at the vegetable varieties they want to grow, consult the month by month planting guide, and make a plan that works for their exact location and situation. A person in this climate can start planting in the greenhouse at least a month earlier than in the planting guide laid out here.

					1	2
3	4	5
6	7	8	9	10	11	12

Plant greens, kales, beets, radishes

first frost

| 13 | 14 | 15 | 16 | 17 | 18 | 19 |

daylength drop below 10 hrs

| 20 | 21 | 22 | 23 | 24 | 25 | 26 |

| 27 | | 29 | 30 | 31 |

Average temp

	H	L
Jan	39	27
Feb	42	29
Mar	50	35
Apr	61	45
May	73	56
Jun	80	64
Jul	86	77
Aug	84	61
Sep	78	63
Oct	66	53
Nov	59	45
Dec	45	35

Zone 7
220 days in growing season

SEED STARTER CHART

by temperature

MIN 35°F

	Best °F	Max °F	#Days
Parsnip	65	85	14
Spinach	70	86	5
Lettuce	75	85	3
Onion	75	95	6

MIN 40°F

	Best °F	Max °F	#Days
Celery	70	85	7
Leek	70	90	7
Parsley	75	90	13
Pea	75	85	6
Cabbage	80	100	4
Carrot	80	95	6
Cauliflower	80	100	5
Kohlrabi	80	90	4
Beets	85	95	4
Radish	85	95	4
Swiss Chard	85	95	4
Turnip	85	105	3

MIN 50°F

	Best °F	Max °F	#Days
Asparragus	75	95	10
Tomato	80	95	6
Sweetcorn	95	105	3

MIN 60°F

	Best °F	Max °F	#Days
Bean, Snap	80	95	7
Eggplant	85	95	6
Bean, Lima	85	85	6
Pepper	85	95	8
Muskmelon	90	100	4
Cucumber	95	105	3
Okra	95	105	6
Pumpkin	95	100	4
Squash	95	100	4
Watermelon	95	105	4
Chicory	80	-	6

MIN 70°F

	Best °F	Max °F	#Days
Brussel Sprouts	80	-	4
Endive	80	-	6

MIN 75°F

	Best °F	Max °F	#Days
Ch. Cabbage	80	-	4
Kale	80	-	4
Rutabaga	80	-	4
Broccoli	85	90	4

Chapter 4

GREENHOUSE GARDENING

Month by Month Planting Guide

The wonderful thing about greenhouse growing is growing food and flowers year-round. It takes some planning to be successful; this isn't something you can do on the fly, but it is entirely worth the effort to have fresh vegetables all year.

Having fresh-grown vegetables is beneficial to your mental and physical health, plus they always taste better. Greenhouses allow gardeners to extend the growing season to enjoy fresh foods and bright flowers even when it's cold and dreary outside.

UNHEATED GREENHOUSE

month by month planting guide

This greenhouse growing calendar is designed for an unheated greenhouse in zone 5, with the use of row covers and mulch to protect against cold. If you live in a different zone, check out the suggestions at the end of this guide.

JANUARY

January is usually the coldest month of the year. If there is no heating, very few vegetables or herbs will make it through the month. Greens such as kale, spinach, and bok choy may be strong enough to hold onto their already grown leaves if they are adequately mulched or covered. This means you can still harvest in January, but you won't be growing anything new.

Onions are the only seeds to start in January. See the instructions in the chapter on Winter Gardening Onions, Potatoes, and Garlic.

The best thing to do in January is plan for the upcoming year. Make sure you have everything you need because once the season gets into full swing, you may find yourself short on time for the menial tasks.

WHAT TO PLANT IN JANUARY:

- Onions

JANUARY GARDENING TASKS:

- If you store your potting soil outside, bring it indoors to warm up before planting any seeds in it. Planting seeds in cold soil will not provide the good start they need.
- Order or buy the seeds you want; don't procrastinate on that.
- Seed shortages are becoming a common occurrence, and if you want something in particular, you need to order early.
- Check all your equipment – spades, shovels, gloves, potting containers, watering cans. Are they clean? Do you have enough? Does anything need repairing?
- Gather mulch, row covers, and hoops to protect young seedlings and quicken germination of early started vegetables.
- Heavily mulch planting beds or top with row covers to warm the soil before planting in February.

FEBRUARY

The early spring, from February to March, often experiences wide temperature fluctuations, which cause problems with greenhouse plants. Bright, beautiful sunny days mixed with extremely cold nights are challenging for fragile seedlings. You may need to heat the greenhouse in the evening, so it stays between 50 and 65°F (10-18C). A passive heat source helps a lot with maintaining these temperatures.

If you have raised beds, it's easier to plant in these because the soil retains heat longer. Heavy mulching, humidity domes, and mini hoop tunnels covered with cloth are also very effective. Keep a close eye on the forecast and use a heat source during the frigid evenings or hold off planting until the temperatures even out. Also, make sure all the vents, windows, and doors work correctly so you can air out the greenhouse as needed.

WHAT TO PLANT IN FEBRUARY IF THE SOIL IS WARM ENOUGH:

- Quick cool-season crops: carrots, beets, peas, radishes, greens (kale, lettuce, spinach, mustard, collards, bok choy)
- Slow cool-season crops: broccoli, cauliflower, cabbage
- Warm-season crops with long seasons: tomatoes, eggplants, peppers, okra
- Start potatoes (see the section on Winter Gardening Onions and Potatoes)

The warm weather plants need a long head start to be successful. They do not tolerate any cold weather. Most of these warm weather vegetables need 100-150 days to mature, and the early boost in the greenhouse means they'll be more successful in the garden later.

To germinate, tomato, eggplant, pepper, and okra seeds require soil temperatures between 55 and 65°F (13-18C). This may not be possible without heating pads or thick mulching. A soil temperature gauge comes in really handy in these instances. Mulch the soil for a couple of weeks before planting to get it as warm as possible. The benefit of this extra seed starting effort is fresh, mature tomatoes as early as June.

When the nighttime temperatures reach over 55°F (13C) consistently, these warm weather crops can be moved outside or allowed to continue growing in the greenhouse.

All the quick cool-season crops can be planted directly in the greenhouse soil or raised beds. To germinate, the seeds need soil temperatures of at least 40°F (4C). Or, you can sow them in seed starting trays, then transplant them to the ground once they are 2-3 inches tall (5-8cm). Carrots however, don't fare well with transplanting, so always put those directly in the ground. Cover all the seedlings with cloth covers or add straw mulch to warm the soil. This helps regulate the fluctuating temperatures and keeps the plants from freezing.

MARCH

Daylight is lengthening, and the greenhouse is going to get busy quickly. Plan carefully, so you don't run out of room later on. Plan on some successive planting; planting greens and carrots a second time so you'll have continuous harvests instead of large gaps between crops.

This is the time to start warm-season crops with shorter days to maturation. These will grow quickly in the greenhouse and be ready for transplanting to raised beds or outside as soon as the temperatures rise.

WHAT TO PLANT IN MARCH:

- Warm-season crops with short seasons: basil, cucumbers, summer squash, kohlrabi
- Quick cold-season crops second planting: carrots, beets, peas, radishes, greens (kale, lettuce, spinach, mustard, collards, bok choy)
- Corn, winter squash, melons
- Potatoes plant chitted (see the section on Winter Gardening Onions and Potatoes)
- Potatoes – start another set (see the section on Winter Gardening Onions and Potatoes)

HARVEST:

- The first crop of cold-hardy vegetables – greens, radishes, baby beets

APRIL

As the soil temperatures slowly start to rise, it is time to move the slow-growing cold-season crops from the greenhouse to the garden. When the nighttime temperature outside is consistently above 45 degrees (7C), transfer the broccoli, cabbage, cauliflower, lettuce, kale, and greens to the garden.

Do a second planting of the warm-season crops that mature quickly, such as beans and cucumbers. We recommend planting 3-6 plants of each type for three months to create a successive harvest. This is ideal for smaller greenhouses that can't support 15-30 plants of each type all at once. Plus, it's easier come harvest time and means much less food goes to waste.

It can be overwhelming dealing with 10 cucumber plants all producing fruit at the same time – you have to pick them all when they're ripe and use them soon after so they don't spoil. This means processing them all, eating them all, or giving them away. When you plan out successive harvests, you only have a few plants to manage at a time which makes harvesting much more manageable. Of course, plan it how it works best for your circumstances.

Onion sets can be planted as soon as the ground is workable.

WHAT TO PLANT IN APRIL:

- Quick cool-weather crops – third planting of carrots, beets, all the greens, radishes
- Warm-season crops with short seasons, second planting: beans, basil, cucumbers, summer squash, kohlrabi
- Potatoes – second planting
- Onion sets
- Dill, mint

HARVEST:

- Carrots, beets, greens, peas, radishes

MAY

When the nighttime temperatures are regularly over 55°F (13C), it's time to move all the warm weather plants out to the garden – tomatoes, peppers, eggplant, beans, squash, pumpkins, cucumbers, watermelon, sunflowers, and corn.

Alternatively, all these warm-weather crops can also stay in the greenhouse all summer long. They'll love the greenhouse, but in the extreme heat of the summer, they'll need lots of watering, venting, and general protection from the heat.

The benefit of keeping these crops in the greenhouse is that they will produce longer because they are more protected from cold and frost later on. If you think tomato season is too short, this is a great way to extend it. Another option is to grow the tomatoes in pots, move them outdoors in the summer, then move them back into the greenhouse before it gets too cold. If you utilize one of the residual heating methods, it should be enough to keep the tomatoes producing for another month.

If you have perennial herbs overwintering in the greenhouse, uncover and water them. New growth should start soon.

WHAT TO PLANT IN MAY:

- Warm-season crops with short seasons, third planting: beans, basil, cucumbers, squash, kohlrabi
- Dill
- Start, or waken, perennial herbs: mint, rosemary, thyme, oregano, sage

HARVEST:

- Greens, kale, peas, spinach, radishes, carrots, beets
- Potatoes might be ready by the end of May, depending on the type.

JUNE

The greenhouse really starts heating up around June. The sun is beating down all day, and it can get too hot for even the warm-season crops. If you've kept the tomatoes, peppers, and okra in the greenhouse instead of planting outside, monitor for overheating. You'll need excellent ventilation to combat stuffy conditions. Plus, you'll need to water more often.

WHAT TO PLANT IN JUNE:

- Potatoes - start another set (see the section on Winter Gardening Onions and Potatoes)

HARVEST:

- Greens, radishes, carrots, beets, peas, potatoes, early tomatoes, basil, dill, mint, rosemary, oregano, sage, thyme

POTATOES:

- Chit another set of potatoes in June for a July planting. Choose a short-season or mid-season variety to ensure they mature before the first frosts. In the greenhouse, you'll be able to extend their growing season by covering the plants and using alternative warming techniques.

JULY

In July, keep an eye on any warm-season crops in the greenhouse. It's too hot for anything except those heat lovers, and even they need vents open and regular, frequent watering.

WHAT TO PLANT IN JULY:

- Potatoes

HARVEST:

- Cucumbers, beans, peppers, carrots, greens, corn, early tomatoes, squash, kohlrabi, basil, dill, mint, rosemary, oregano, sage, thyme

POTATOES

- Cut seed potatoes, let them heal over, then plant in large grow bags or raised garden beds. Grow bags are convenient since they are maneuverable until they get too heavy. Keep the bags in the coolest location in the greenhouse, as the seed potatoes don't like hot dirt and ensure the greenhouse is well vented.

AUGUST

It's time to start thinking about the winter garden! That's right, in the heat of summer, you need to plan so you'll have maturing crops before it's too cold to grow anything. The goal is to have the winter crops mature before the end of November. Crops go into a sort of hibernation as the weather cools and stop producing new growth, but they don't die. These plants remain viable and alive; they just aren't creating new leaves, fruits, or roots. So, you want these crops to be fully matured before it gets too cold, and then they'll overwinter in the greenhouse, and you can harvest at will.

WHAT TO PLANT IN AUGUST:

- Quick cool-season crops: radishes, beets, kale, greens, parsley, chives, scallions, carrots
- Quick warm-season crops: beans
- Garlic, so it will overwinter – wait until soil temp is down to around 60°F (16C)

HARVEST:

- Tomatoes, peppers, cucumbers, squash, okra, eggplant, corn, melons, broccoli, cauliflower, onions, basil, dill, mint, rosemary, oregano, sage, thyme

SEPTEMBER

This month is devoted to harvesting all the summer crops. The greenhouse winter garden will need constant watching to ensure it doesn't get too hot and stress the plants. You can also do a second planting of quick cool-season crops.

WHAT TO PLANT IN SEPTEMBER:

- Greens, radishes, beets, kale

HARVEST:

- Tomatoes, peppers, cucumbers, squash, corn, okra, eggplant, melons, potatoes, broccoli, cabbage, cauliflower, onions, basil, dill, mint, rosemary, sage, thyme, oregano

Move any sensitive fruit trees into the greenhouse before the first frost arrives. Fruits such as citrus and figs, and potted vegetables, such as peppers and tomatoes, can survive a bit longer in the greenhouse.

OCTOBER

October is mainly devoted to maintaining the winter greenhouse garden. Do another small planting of quick cool-season crops if you've got the space. These likely won't reach full maturity, but young greens are always tender and delicious.

WHAT TO PLANT IN OCTOBER:

- Greens, radishes

HARVEST:

- Greens, potatoes, beets, pumpkins, winter squash, carrots, onions, beans, dill, mint, sage, thyme, oregano, rosemary

Kale, spinach, and lettuce still have time to develop into small plants before it gets too cold. They'll overwinter Nov-Feb, then start growing rapidly as the days lengthen. This is a fun and rewarding way to get a head start on fresh greens in winter.

Fun Fact: Winter vegetables store sugars in their cells to protect against frost, making them taste sweeter – an absolute delight.

NOVEMBER

There's not much that will plant well in November. You may be able to squeeze in an extra crop of lettuce and spinach, but they probably won't grow large – that's fine though. Baby spinach and early lettuce are delicious.

Move all the perennial herbs indoors to overwinter – cut them back and protect the roots as described in the Herbs Winter Growing section.

HARVEST:

- Greens, radishes, beets, kale, mint

DECEMBER

December is about maintaining the winter garden, monitoring temperatures, and harvesting whatever is available. This is also a great time to start thinking about next year's garden. Think of what worked and didn't work and what changes should be made.

HARVEST:

- Greens, radishes, beets, kale

Adjust this planting schedule to fit your greenhouse and your tastes. You don't have to grow everything; plant what you like and enjoy having fresh vegetables year-round.

Also, feel free to experiment by starting vegetables earlier (or later) and see how they do. And don't worry if there are failures. Even the most experienced gardeners have setbacks. One of the joys of greenhouse gardening is trying new things and seeing how they turn out.

TIPS FOR A SUCCESSFUL WINTER GREENHOUSE:

- Plant directly in the ground or in raised beds. Avoid planting in small containers, as the soil in them will freeze faster than the ground or raised beds.
- Plan it out in advance.
- Keep the water source inside the greenhouse, possibly heated, so you're not fighting with ice every time you need to water.
- Water less frequently – winter watering is vastly different from summer watering. Winter greenhouse crops don't dry out as fast; monitor the soil to only water when it is dry. Make sure you only water in the morning so the plants can dry out a bit before cold nighttime temperatures hit.
- Cover the bare soil in late fall and winter to heat up the earth for winter planting. Do this for a couple of weeks before planting seeds, and continue after planting.

AMENDMENTS FOR OTHER ZONES

In the hot south, move up the calendar, so you are starting in September. This gives you time to grow everything before the real heat of summer starts and everything wilts. By January and February, you'll be harvesting fresh vegetables.

As mentioned before, the greenhouse climate is naturally 10 degrees Fahrenheit (6 degrees Celsius) higher than the outside temperature. This creates a very hot environment, but one that can be utilized to grow tropical plants, such as papaya or bananas. A summer greenhouse in a hot climate can still grow tomatoes, eggplants, and other heat-loving vegetables and herbs, as long as the temperature is monitored. In general, anything over 90°F (32°C) is dangerous for vegetable plants.

To grow anything during the summer months other than tropicals, you'll need to use extensive shade cloths, set up cooling systems, make good use of vents and doors for a breeze, and never neglect to water. Many southern greenhouse growers set up hydroponic systems to alleviate the constant need for water.

Another method to mitigate heat is to grow tall tropical plants such as bananas or plumeria, and once they are tall enough, they will provide a natural canopy to shade plants beneath it.

Planting year-round in the greenhouse is a phenomenal way to access fresh vegetables throughout every season. It does take some planning at first, which may seem overwhelming. However, it will go much smoother once you do it for a year or two. Don't worry if you have setbacks – that's how we, as gardeners learn. Just pick up the seeds and soil and try again. The greenhouse is a gardener's playground! We hope this month-by-month plan makes the process much easier and that your greenhouse teems with vegetables all year.

WHAT TO START

JAN	FEB	MAR	APR	MAY	JUN
Onions	Greens (Bok choy, chard, kale, spinach, mustard) Carrots Beets Peas Broccoli Cabbage Cauliflower Tomato Eggplant Okra Peppers Radishes Potatoes	Lettuce- Greens Kohlrabi Summer Squash Basil Cucumbers Lettuce Beets Radishes Peas Corn Winter Squash Melons Potatoes	Lettuce- Greens Kale Radishes Carrots Beets Beans Basil Cucumbers Summer Squash Kohlrabi Potatoes Dill Mint Onions Peas	Beans Basil Cucumbers Summer Squash Kohlrabi Dill Perennial Herbs	Potatoes

JUL	AUG	SEP	OCT	NOV	DEC
Potatoes	Lettuce- Greens Beets Radishes Parsley Carrots Beans Garlic	Lettuce- Greens Beets Radishes	Lettuce- Greens Beets Radishes	Lettuce- Greens Beets Radishes	Nothing

WHAT TO HARVEST

JAN	FEB	MAR	APR	MAY	JUN
Greens	Greens	Greens Radishes Baby Beets	Greens Beets Carrots Radishes Peas	Greens Peas Carrots Beets	Greens Radishes Carrots Beets Peas Tomatoes Herbs Potatoes

JUL	AUG	SEP	OCT	NOV	DEC
Cucumbers Beans Peppers Corn Tomatoes Summer Squash Greens Carrots Kohlrabi Herbs Potatoes	Cucumbers Beans Peppers Corn Tomatoes Summer Squash Greens Carrots Kohlrabi Okra Eggplant Melons Broccoli Cauliflower Onions Herbs Potatoes	Cucumbers Beans Peppers Corn Tomatoes Summer Squash Greens Carrots Kohlrabi Okra Eggplant Melons Broccoli Cauliflower Onions Herbs Potatoes	Pumpkins Winter Squash Carrots Onions Beans Greens Potatoes Beets Herbs	Greens Radishes Beets Mint	Greens Radishes Beets

Chapter 5

GARDENING BY TYPE OF Vegetable, Fruit and Herb

HOW TO GROW VEGETABLES

in a greenhouse

Knowing what type of greenhouse climate your vegetables prefer will lead you on the path to success. Vegetables aren't one homogeneous group; each species has its preferences for light, watering, temperature, and climate. Even though the growing calendar instructs when to plant each vegetable, knowing their individual preferences will assist you in choosing the exact best time to grow them in your greenhouse.

All the containers you will be using to plant the seeds should be sterilized. This is to ensure the greenhouse remains a clean environment. It would be awful to transport diseases or pests into the enclosed area of a greenhouse where they can spread quickly. A solution of one part bleach to nine parts water is good. Soak the containers for ten minutes, then rinse in clean water and dry.

You can also use apple cider vinegar in place of bleach. If you're using Styrofoam planting plugs, a good washing with a hose or pressure washer is great. Also, they can be soaked in a garbage can and then rinsed. Whichever method you use to clean your containers, make sure they are washed thoroughly afterwards and dried completely as bleach and vinegar can have a detrimental effect on seeds.

SHORT COOL SEASON VEGETABLES

Asian Greens (Bok Choy, Mizuna, Mustards, Sensopai)

Asian greens are cold-hardy and can be started in early spring in the greenhouse, any time between February and April. Plan on planting a new set every 3-4 weeks for a continuous harvest through the spring. Plant in starter trays and then transplant to raised beds or directly into the ground when they are 3-4 inches (8-10 centimeters) tall. Or start them in containers and leave them there.

The great thing about Asian greens is that they are fast growers. This means you'll have young greens to harvest in 30 days. Once it starts to get hot out, the greens will bolt and won't taste good anymore. So, be sure to gather all the spring-planted Asian greens before they start bolting.

For a winter crop of Asian greens, start seeds in the greenhouse in August and September. They can be sown directly in the ground, raised beds, or containers. Starting them in late summer gives the plants time to reach maturity before freezing weather starts. Even when it's cold outside, the plants will overwinter if covered during the coldest times. Use shade cloth or straw to mulch around the plants and warm up their roots.

The best part about Asian greens is that the overwintered plants will burst into production once spring returns.

Beets

The versatility of beets makes them an ideal greenhouse vegetable, especially in cool climates. Beets can be grown for their bulbs or just their greens. Start beets in the greenhouse when the soil temperature is at least 40°F (4C). They can be started directly in the greenhouse soil, in containers with enough depth for the roots, or starter plugs.

Beets reach maturity in 45-60 days, depending on the type. Choose shorter season varieties for a quicker spring harvest. Beets planted in February will germinate slowly since the soil is still chilly. Use row covers or mulch to warm the soil and quicken germination and growth.

Those planted in September, October, or November will germinate quicker but may not have enough time to reach full maturity. This is fine, though, since the greens and small bulbs are edible.

Kale, Collards, Chard

Kale survives down to 10°F (-12C) , which is phenomenal for the cold winter garden. At that temperature, they won't grow, but they won't die either. So, you can continue harvesting the greens. Kale actually tastes better after it's experienced a frost or two – it sweetens the taste.

Choose kale, collard green, and Swiss chard varieties based on where you live – extreme cold-hardy types or heat adaptable types. In general, these fast-growing greens suffer significantly in heat. Often, they will wilt and die back but may revive again if temperatures decrease.

Start planting kale, collards, and Swiss chard in February as seed starts to be transplanted to raised beds, the greenhouse floor, or containers. Do successive plantings until May, when the temperatures begin to warm, and any new plants will have to fight the summer. Plant again for the winter garden, and you'll have plenty of greens throughout the year.

Kohlrabi

Plant kohlrabi directly in the greenhouse floor, in raised beds, or pots when the soil temperature is at least 40°F (4C). Kohlrabi likes cooler weather, but exposure to frost will cause it to bolt. Use row covers in the early spring greenhouse to keep it protected.

In August, direct seed in the greenhouse for a crop before extreme cold hits. Kohlrabi is ready to harvest in as little as six weeks.

Lettuce

As long as the temperature is above 45°F (7C), lettuce will do really well in a greenhouse environment. Even an unheated greenhouse will be okay. When the temperature gets hot though, lettuce and other greens don't do well. This is a cool-season crop. Leaf lettuce tolerates heat better than head lettuce.

Lettuce can be planted in containers, or if you have a dirt floor, they can be seeded directly into the soil. They need full sun, so choose a spot in the greenhouse where they will get at least six hours of direct sunlight.

Fill containers with a good soil-less potting mix and soak with water. The soil-less potting mixes don't absorb water well at first, so it will take a few passes with the hose to get them completely wet. Plant seeds 1/4-1/2" deep and 1" apart. The seeds will take 35-45 days to mature and be ready for harvest. The soil should be kept moist but not waterlogged.

The greenhouse should be kept between 50°F (10C) and 70°F (21C). Any higher than this and the lettuce will wilt. If it is too warm, open vents and doors to keep the temperature down. The nighttime temperature is best if it is between 45°F (7C) and 55°F (13C). A few colder nights won't kill the lettuce, and a few extra hot days won't hurt it either but try to minimize that as much as possible.

Lettuce actually has an interesting survival technique for freezing temperatures. When the temperature drops, the lettuce plants relocate water out of their cells into the intercellular spaces to ensure the freezing temperature doesn't destroy the cell walls. When this happens, their leaves will go limp, and it will look like the entire crop has died off. However, as soon as they are in sunlight and the greenhouse warms up, they re-hydrate and look alive again.

Lettuce can be harvested directly in the greenhouse. It doesn't need to be transplanted outside; however, it can be if desired. To harvest lettuce, cut the leaves off when they are 3-6" tall. Cut them 1/2" above the stem, and they will regrow again and again. It is possible to harvest four or five times before the plant is spent.

Lettuce can also be grown in the winter. It will take longer to germinate and mature, usually 50-80 days instead of 45 days, yet it is worth it to have freshly grown lettuce in the middle of winter. See the section about winter crop growing for more information.

Peas

A cool weather vegetable, peas do well in a greenhouse. Even in wintertime, they are truly an all-season vegetable when you have a greenhouse. The two main varieties of peas are snow peas and snap peas. Both have the same growing requirements and can thrive in a greenhouse space. Peas are winter crops, but still some places are too cold for them. There are cold-resistant varieties that fare better in places with snow and freezing temperatures.

A greenhouse can be used to grow peas at almost any time of year. They can be started in a greenhouse in early spring and then transplanted to the garden after the threat of frost has passed. Early autumn, early winter, and late winter are all possibilities as well. The only time peas don't like to grow is in the intense heat of the summer sun. In fall and winter, the peas will grow entirely in the greenhouse. They will take a bit of setting up and a bunch of patience, yet it is entirely worth it for fresh peas. They will take longer to germinate and grow in the depth of cold weather. Usually, peas take 50-55 days to get to maturity. In winter, this is extended to 3-4 months.

To grow peas for a winter garden, start them in late September. Use a rich soil-less potting mix for best results. Fill the containers and then water the potting mix, so it is thoroughly moist. It takes a little while for it to absorb water, and so it may take a few passes. Plant the seeds 1" deep.

The soil should be always moist but don't let it get waterlogged. Set the containers in a place where they can drain well. The soil temperature needs to be at least 40°F (4C) for the seeds to germinate. If it is colder than that in your area, using a heating mat under the containers will work well. Several layers of frost blankets placed over the seeds is another option that has worked well for many gardeners in cold locations.

Once the seeds have sprouted, they need a daytime temperature of around 75°F (24C). Since there isn't as much sun in winter, the seedlings may need you to provide them with more heat. It depends on how warm it gets in your greenhouse during the day. A thermometer is a good tool to have in the greenhouse for this reason. If it is particularly cold where you live, leaving several layers of frost blankets over the peas should give them the heat they need.

They need a minimum of six hours of sunlight per day. They will do better if they receive more. If you add grow lamps, they should be adjustable so as the plant grows they can be moved upwards to accommodate this. The light should be placed no more than two feet above the plant.

When the seedlings reach 5" tall, transplant them to larger pots. Put a trellis, at least three feet high, in the pot behind the plant. Carefully wrap the shoots around the trellis and encourage them as they grow, to use the trellis for support. Handle the plant carefully as it has a shallow root system and can be pulled up easily.

Pick the pea pods as they become ready. This will encourage further production, and you can be eating fresh pea pods for quite a while.

Radishes

One of the best winter vegetable crops, radishes are super-fast growing and like cool temperatures. The soil temperature needs to be at least 55°F (13C) for them to germinate, so you may need to warm the soil a bit before spring planting. Once they get established, though, they'll do fine in cooler weather.

Radishes are frost tolerant, and most are ready for harvest in 30-45 days. And they don't take up much space. Do as many plantings as you want, from February through May, before the greenhouse gets too warm for them.

Then, in August and September, plant them for the winter garden. Again, do as many consecutive plantings as you like. Radishes are easy to grow in raised beds, the greenhouse floor, or pots. They can also fit into unused spaces, easily tucked into corners.

LONG COOL SEASON VEGETABLES

Broccoli, Cabbage, and Cauliflower

These cruciferous vegetables are cold-tolerant and need a long growing season. Primarily, they need to get started when it is cool out so they can reach maturity before the blazing summer hits and they all bolt.

Sow broccoli, cabbage, and cauliflower seeds in February or March, when the soil temperature is at least 40°F (4C). Mulching or covering the planted seeds will help speed up germination.

Carrots

Carrots will germinate in temperatures as low as 35-45°F (2-7C). They won't germinate quickly, and they're notoriously slow to begin with, but this means it's possible to grow carrots all winter long. The carrots will slowly grow as long as the soil temperature is above 35°F (2C).

Carrots are versatile cool-season crops, but they don't like excessive heat. Plan to mature all your greenhouse carrots before it gets overly warm inside. Plant them in the ground or raised beds. They also grow well in containers.

This root vegetable does not like to be transplanted, so plant it where you want it to grow. Carrots are excellent greenhouse vegetables because they don't take up a lot of room and can be planted densely. February plantings of carrots like having row covers to accelerate germination and growth.

Chives

This herb is a perennial, which means it will grow back every year if the conditions are right. Chives prefer cooler weather; heat makes them wilt and bolt. Planting chives in containers is useful so you can move them indoors and outdoors with the temperature. During extreme freezes, the foliage will die back – it's best to cut it all off when you see that happen. As soon as the temperature is amenable again, they'll sprout.

In the greenhouse, chives do well planted with carrots. Plant them directly in the soil, raised beds, or pots. You only need one planting to have chives the entire year.

SHORT WARM SEASON VEGETABLES

Beans (Bush and Pole)

Plant beans as soon as the soil temperatures are at least 60°F (16C). Sow them directly in the greenhouse, in raised beds or containers since those will probably be able to maintain a slightly higher soil temperature. Beans do not transplant well, and they grow quickly, so there isn't much need for starting them early.

April and May are the best time in spring to plant beans. Do several plantings to have continuous harvests.

Then, sow another set in late summer before the temperatures start to cool down, so you'll have a late-season crop. Beans will not overwinter in a cold greenhouse; the plants are too tender. You can start the late summer beans in pots outside, then bring them into the greenhouse as the days begin to cool, to extend their growing season.

Cucumbers

Cucumbers are not frost tolerant. They need warm soil to germinate and warm soil to grow. The great thing is that they grow quickly. Start seeds in the greenhouse in April or May, then transplant directly into the greenhouse ground, into raised beds, containers, or to the outdoor garden. Cucumbers are a wonderful spring and summer greenhouse crop because they don't take up much room when trellised.

Plant them in a pot next to a support pole and tie them up as they grow. They'll thrive in the greenhouse warmth. Excessive heat, anything over 95°F (35C), will stop their growth though, so be sure the greenhouse is well-ventilated in summer.

Summer Squash and Zucchini

Plant squash seeds in the greenhouse to give them a head start. This isn't always necessary since they are fast-growing plants anyway, but it's nice to have zucchini early. Start 2-4 plants in March and then a couple more in April. Remember, squash plants produce abundantly, so you only need a few.

Summer squash needs a minimum 60°F (16C) soil temperature to germinate. Warm the soil with row covers or use propagation mats. Then, after planting, give the seeds plenty of warmth and lots of light. Covering the seedlings at night will help keep them warm.

Zucchini and summer squash aren't ideal greenhouse crops because they are so large.

Use the greenhouse to start seeds, or grow them in deep, wide containers which can be moved outside. Squash depends on beneficial insects for pollinating and won't set fruit if it lacks pollination.

LONG WARM SEASON VEGETABLES

Corn

Corn isn't the best greenhouse crop unless you have the space for it. It grows quite tall, takes up lots of room, and relies on wind pollination. Part of the issue is that to pollinate correctly, corn needs to be planted in blocks of 10-12. You can't just plant one corn. For most home greenhouse growers, corn isn't viable in the greenhouse as a full-time plant.

Doing corn seed starts in spring gives a decent head start on the season though. Many gardeners, even professionals, warn against seed-starting corn because it doesn't transplant well. It can be a little hit or miss, but to get an extra jump on corn on the cob season it is absolutely worth it. Start a flat of corn seeds in March for planting out in the garden as soon as the soil temperature is above 50°F (10C).

Eggplant & Okra

These heat-loving vegetables need soil temperatures of at least 60°F (16C) to germinate and lots of sun to grow. Their season is usually 5-6 months. This isn't an issue for southern growers, and eggplant and okra will have plenty of time to reach maturity. They'll need a good head start in colder climates to get even close to maturity and a harvest.

A greenhouse is an incredible tool for growing these two crops. Start them as early as February if you can keep the soil warm enough for them to germinate. Row covers and passive heat are usually necessary.

Both eggplant and okra are best sown as seed starts to be transplanted or planted directly in a raised bed if there is space. They are also both tall plants, so make sure there will be enough room for the matured versions.

As soon as day-lengths decrease, the lack of light will slow the plants down considerably. If you plant them in containers, they can be moved outside during the summer then brought indoors once it gets chilly to extend their harvest season. This is best for pollination, too.

Peppers

Just about every variety of pepper will grow well in a greenhouse. There are many types to choose from, sweet peppers to hot peppers, and they will all thrive in your greenhouse environment. The temperature at night must be above 55°F (13C) for them to grow well. This will require waiting until the temperature outside is high enough to start them or ensuring that you have a heat source you can turn on at night to help them out.

Choose a variety that grows tall instead of growing outwards and becoming bushy. Space is usually at a premium in a greenhouse, and so it is best to choose those that aren't going to take up a lot of room. The plants need to be spaced appropriately, or diseases can bloom.

Peppers are slow to germinate. Getting a head start on the growing season by starting the seedlings in the greenhouse will make a huge difference in how soon they are ready to harvest. Pepper seeds need warm soil and being in the controlled atmosphere of a greenhouse is perfect for them. When the outside temperatures are high enough for planting outside, you will have strong, sturdy seedlings ready to transplant.

Seven to ten weeks before the date you want to move the seedlings to the garden, plant the seeds in the greenhouse. The planned date to move them to the garden should be around two-three weeks after the last expected frost. Transplanting seedlings directly after the last expected frost is too chancy since there is still the possibility of a frost occurring. It is unlikely the pepper plants would make it through a frost. Therefore, giving a few weeks of buffer time is ideal.

Fill the planting containers with a soil-less mix designed for seed starting. These mixes are readily available at garden centers. Water the soil until it is moist and cohesive. Soil-less mixes are difficult to soak at first, so it will likely take a few passes to get it totally wet.

Make a 1/2" indentation on the top of the soil and place the pepper seed inside. Cover the seeds lightly with soil. Place a layer of clear plastic wrap over the containers to increase the warmth inside. The soil needs to be between 65°F-95°F (18-35C) to germinate. If your greenhouse is not heated, you'll need to place heat mats underneath the pots to bring the temperature up.

Seedlings will emerge in eight days to three weeks, depending on the warmth of the soil and the type of pepper. Hot pepper varieties take longer to germinate. When the plants start to come up, take off the plastic wrap and move them to an area in the greenhouse that gets a lot of light.

The seedlings will grow better if the daytime temperature is between 65°F-70°F (18-21C) during the day and 60°F-65°F (16-18C) at night. You may need to add heat to your greenhouse to maintain these temperatures. When the seedlings have developed their first set of leaves, thin them if necessary or transplant them to larger pots so they have more room to grow.

Water your pepper plants regularly and fertilize them with a water-soluble mixture once or twice a week. It is helpful for strengthening the plant to let the soil dry out between waterings. The soil should be watered until it is moist but not soaked.

A week before you intend to plant the peppers in the garden (when the soil temperature outdoors is consistently reaching at least 65°F (18C)), harden them off. This entails removing them from the greenhouse and setting them outside in a protected place for a couple of hours each day to get them acclimated to the outdoor conditions. Gradually extend the time they are left out. Plant the peppers in your garden in a location that gets full sun.

Melons (Watermelon, Cantaloupe, Muskmelon)

All melons are heat-loving crops. Start seeds for transplanting in March or April, so they're well-established by the time it's warm enough outside for them. You'll need to warm the soil to at least 60°F (16C) for them to germinate correctly in the unheated greenhouse. Use seed heating mats or row covers to warm the soil beforehand.

Melons grow wonderfully in a warm greenhouse, but they also take up a lot of space. The long vines and large fruit are challenging to manage in a greenhouse, especially a small one. Melons are not the best choice for greenhouse growing for everyone. Some dwarf varieties are worth investigating, though.

Plant seeds in starter trays, then transplant to larger pots, and then to the garden as the temperature increases. Or, leave in the pots to grow in the greenhouse on a trellis. Melons need to be pollinated, so if you're leaving them in the greenhouse, make sure there are windows or vents for pollinators to come through or else you'll need to do it by hand.

Pumpkins & Winter Squash

These vegetables all need long growing seasons and lots of light and warmth. Starting them in the greenhouse is excellent, as it gives them a good head start. Keeping them in the greenhouse is difficult unless you have the space or ability to trellis them. Many of the fruits get quite large, so trellising gets challenging. There are many dwarf varieties that are worth trying, though.

Tomatoes

Warm up the soil, warm up the greenhouse, and start tomato seeds in February or March. They'll need some extra care to germinate and thrive, but it is absolutely worth it for early June and July tomatoes.

Tomatoes need soil temperatures of at least 60°F (16C) to germinate. Then, once germinated, they like lots of light and 70°F (21C). Use row covers or mulch at night to keep the plants warm – they are not frost tolerant.

Once the greenhouse starts to warm up naturally, the tomatoes will thrive. Keep an eye on watering and ventilation, so they don't get overheated. Choose smaller varieties to keep in the greenhouse and sow larger types for transplanting out to the garden.

Tomatoes grow wonderfully in deep pots, so another option is to move them outdoors for the summer and then back into the greenhouse to continue producing when it starts cooling off.

There are hundreds of tomato varieties to choose from. Pay attention to the days to maturity and make sure it will work with your greenhouse and growing season. Days to maturation range from 65 days for early varieties all the way up to 100 days for long-season types.

HOW TO GROW FRUITS

in a greenhouse

It may be surprising to some that a good variety of fruits can also be grown in a greenhouse. Greenhouses are not just for vegetables. Grapes, peaches, nectarines, plums, figs, and citrus fruits can all thrive in a greenhouse setting. Many don't even need a heated greenhouse. In Europe, greenhouses were called orangeries since they were originally built to grow oranges.

GRAPES

Early fruiting, hardy varieties of grapes do best especially if you are in a colder climate. It isn't necessary to have a heated greenhouse. They will do fine in a cold frame.

Grapes spread out a lot, so before planting them, make sure you have enough room in your greenhouse. A single grapevine is enough for a small greenhouse as it will really spread out. If you have a larger greenhouse, multiple grape vines can be planted three feet apart.

Ideally, the greenhouse can be designed specifically for the purpose of growing grapes to create the optimal conditions. There should be 7-8 feet between the two long walls, so the grapes have enough room to grow. A milky colored polycarbonate glazing is best. Clear glazing materials bring in too much harsh, direct, sunlight. The milky colored glazing lets in enough sun without being overwhelming. Because grape vines will grow high up in the greenhouse, they will be especially susceptible to intense heat.

Grapes need a lot of light to grow, and it is important that the vines can soak up as much sun as possible. The vines should be planted northeast to southwest for the best growth. With this row alignment, the vines will get the first rays of sunshine in the morning.

A well-ventilated greenhouse is best for growing grapes. They like warmth and dryness. Too much humidity will encourage fungal diseases and decrease pollination. In the summer and fall, the greenhouse vents should be kept open.

The vines will grow best if the roots are planted outside of the greenhouse. The vine would then be trained to go into the greenhouse through gaps at ground level. Alternately, they can be planted directly into the soil at the inside edge of the greenhouse. Vines do best planted opposite the door and then trained to go up the side of the wall and along the ridge of the roof towards the door.

Alternately, grape vines can also be grown in containers. The pot will need to be at least 12"-15" in depth and diameter. In a small greenhouse, this may be preferable. Vines planted in the ground will grow prolifically and may overwhelm the greenhouse space. They will need to be constantly pruned to keep them under control. Growing in a container limits the root growth and thus the size of the plant. The other benefit to growing in pots is that they can be moved outside during the cold months. They are hardy and will do fine outside. In late winter or early spring, the pots can be relocated back inside the greenhouse to give the grapes a head start in their fruiting.

Plant the grape vines at the same depth that they are in the pot to lessen their shock. Before planting, add compost or fertilizer to the hole. A good time to plant grapevines is November and December. The vines can be pruned at this time of year without the stress of bleeding. Bleeding is when a tree or vine leaks sap. It can be light or heavy and is often harmless, but messy. Sometimes it is fatal to the vine though.

In the spring, when the foliage starts to grow, apply a fertilizer every three weeks. High potassium fertilizer, like that used for tomatoes is good. Once the leaves are full, increase the fertilizer applications to weekly. Stop the fertilizer when the grapes begin to ripen so as not to negatively affect their flavor.

Every week during the growing season, the vine should be watered. If the vine is planted outside, the weather may help you out with watering. If the vine is inside the greenhouse, you will need to be attentive to the watering schedule. Pollination occurs via the wind, so when it comes time to pollinate, open vents and doors to create a cross-breeze that will allow the wind to flow through. Temperature activated windows are great in this situation. Manual pollination in combination with the wind is ideal. With the greenhouse

THE BEGINNER'S GUIDE TO GREENHOUSE GARDENING *Richard Bay*

vents open, gently shake the vines or cup your hand and brush it over flowers to transfer pollen between the flowers.

Grapes will need to be trellised. Long, sturdy wooden dowels placed across the rafters are an easy solution. Make sure they are strong since grape vines can get quite heavy. Also, pay attention to their height to ensure you won't be running into the vines every time you walk into the greenhouse. A grapevine will send out tendrils in all directions in an effort to support itself against any structure it encounters. Remove them as you see them since they will tangle up with the fruits and also allow the vine to go wherever it pleases. Train the vine to go where you want, so it doesn't overwhelm the greenhouse.

LEMONS AND OTHER CITRUS FRUITS

Lemons are a great choice for greenhouse growing since they require little attention once they are established. Dwarf lemon trees are best for the size of a greenhouse. There are several varieties to choose from, and they produce the same size fruit as larger trees. With the right temperature and climate, a lemon tree can produce fruit all year round.

Citrus trees need lots of warmth which means that if you live in a cold climate, the greenhouse will need to be heated. This will be especially true at night when temperatures really drop. A minimum nighttime temperature of 50°F (10C) is required. The trees won't grow fast, but they will still grow at this temperature. A higher temperature is even better; however, you'll have to determine if the cost of heating is worth it.

Planting the trees in pots is necessary to keep their growth limited. A 10-gallon container is good. Some trees can get quite big and if allowed, will take up your whole greenhouse. A dwarf lemon tree in a pot will grow to between three and five feet. Having them in pots also lets you move them outside during the warm months and then into the protection of the greenhouse once the weather starts to get too cold for them. A lemon tree likes lots of sun so place the pot near the southern end of your greenhouse. To prevent leaf scalding, set it 1'-2' away from the wall glazing. Water the tree whenever the soil feels dry. The pot should be propped up on bricks or stones, so that water can drain out of the bottom. During the winter, watering can decrease to about once a week. A good rule of thumb is to water whenever the leaves look wilted. When the tree is outside, it may need watering every day. Every month, the tree should be fertilized. In the fall, stop fertilizing, so the tree can rest.

Having a thermometer set near your lemon tree will be very useful to maintain the required temperatures. If the temperature falls below 50°F (10C), turn on the heat. If it goes above 95°F (35C), open the ventilation. During the summer months, if you are keeping your lemon tree in the greenhouse, drape a shade cloth along the southern wall of the greenhouse to prevent the tree from getting too much sun.

Citrus trees do not fare well in frost and often die off if exposed to it for too long. They will be okay in a cold, dark location and will become dormant. They can be kept in a cold greenhouse for protection; however, they will not produce fruit in those conditions. They should be surrounded by a light blocking material or kept in a dark corner. Any amount of light tells the tree that it should be growing and producing fruit, and it won't become dormant. A cold greenhouse is not capable of giving the tree all it needs to produce fruit under these conditions. The tree will get confused and drop its leaves and possibly die. Leaf drop happens when the root temperatures get low at the same time as the leaves are receiving light. The plant tries to grow and can't because the roots are cold, and so it drops its leaves.

To keep the tree in the greenhouse and producing fruit during the winter, it needs to receive light and heat.

The trees can be moved outside when the nighttime temperature is above 55F (13C). Put them in a shady spot first so as not to shock them. Too much sun too fast will sunburn them. Move the trees carefully, because in the spring they will have flowers and small fruit that can be knocked off. In the fall, the trees may be full of fruit and too much jostling of the plant could make the fruit fall off.

Pruning is best done in the winter when the tree is partially dormant. Pay attention to spotted or pale leaves which can indicate a thrip infection which is common in lemon trees.

Peaches and nectarines are similar in structure, and the growing requirements for them are basically the same. They won't produce fruit year-round because the tree needs to go dormant and rest. A greenhouse

PEACHES AND NECTARINES

provides a haven for peach and nectarine trees in the winter. The greenhouse should remain unheated, so the tree can go dormant without the worry of frost hurting it.

Choose the soil carefully when planting. Peach trees strongly dislike heavy wet soil. They want well-drained, light soil that can retain moisture without getting bogged down. Neutral and slightly acid soils are best. The pH should not be below 6.5. If it does go that low, treat the base of the tree with lime in the fall. If the acid is too low, the peach pit will not harden, and the center of the fruit will decay.

Plant peaches and nectarines in large pots that can be moved. In the spring, as with lemon trees, they can be moved outside to take advantage of the warmer outside weather. In the late fall, they should be moved back into the greenhouse for protection. Another option is to leave the tree outside all winter and only move it into the greenhouse for a few weeks in early spring to protect the new buds from frost. This will give you a jump start on the season, and you will have fresh peaches sooner.

HOW TO GROW HERBS

in a greenhouse

There are a lot of herbs that will grow well in a greenhouse environment. A greenhouse can protect the herb plants from the intensity of the summer sun. Greenhouses are also a great way to extend the season for growing herbs, so they can grow earlier and later. Chives, cilantro, dill, parsley, basil, lavender, sage, oregano, and chamomile are good choices for greenhouse growing.

Follow the process listed in the section on peppers to clean and sterilize any pots you will be using before bringing them into the greenhouse. Use a high-quality soil-less potting mix to plant the seeds.

BASIL

Basil is simple to grow and does very well in a controlled greenhouse environment. The greenhouse can be used to grow the crop from start to finish or as a place to get a jump start on the season before the seedlings can be transplanted outside.

Water the potting mix thoroughly before planting the seeds. Make a 1/2" indentation in the potting soil and place the seeds in. Cover them lightly with the potting mix. If you have a greenhouse with a dirt floor, basil can be planted directly in the ground.

To germinate, basil seeds need to be around 70°F (21C). If your greenhouse is not heated, the containers will need to be placed on heating pads. Covering the top with a layer of clear plastic wrap will help keep the temperature up until they germinate. Once the seedlings start to show, remove the plastic wrap. If the seedlings are in starter plugs, they should be transplanted to 4" pots.

Basil seedlings are prone to damping off which is a fungal disease caused by the roots being over-watered and remaining damp for too long. After they've grown a bit, water the basil plants once a week, letting the soil dry out between watering. Over-watering will cause the bottom leaves to turn yellow. Ideally, basil needs six-eight hours of full sun per day to thrive. Depending on your greenhouse setup, you may need to add additional heat and lighting during cool seasons with less sun.

On hot summer days, make use of the greenhouse ventilation. Basil can easily die from overheating.

If the seedlings are being transplanted to your garden, harden them off beforehand. Set them outside for a couple of hours one day and then slowly increase the time they spend outside. Taking them straight from a heated greenhouse to the garden will shock them, and the plants will suffer and may not survive.

When the plants are 6-8" tall, they are ready to be harvested. Harvest basil by pinching off the leaves. The plant will continue to grow and produce for quite a while if you continuously harvest it.

PARSLEY AND CILANTRO

Like basil, parsley and cilantro can be planted in pots, raised beds, or directly into the ground if you have a dirt floor in your greenhouse.

Parsley is very slow to germinate and can take up to a month. To speed up the process, soak the seeds in very warm water (110°F/43C) overnight before planting. Remove any seeds that float. Plant the seeds immediately and be sure to keep the soil moist until the seeds sprout.

They should be planted 1/4-1/2" in the soil. A good method for doing this is by pressing the seed into the soil to the correct depth. This is easier than making tiny holes to plant each seed into. Cover the tray or pots with plastic wrap to keep the soil warm and moist. Once the seeds sprout, remove the plastic wrap.

Parsley seeds do not fare well in cool temperatures. If you are cultivating them to be transplanted into your garden, plant them just two-three weeks before the last expected frost in your area. A cold frame greenhouse may need heating pads underneath the pots to keep the seedlings warm. The optimal growing temperature for parsley is between 65°-75°F (18-24C). A heated greenhouse or the use of heating mats is especially beneficial for parsley seedlings.

Set the pots up in a way that they can drain easily. Parsley likes to be well watered, yet it isn't good to flood them.

Once parsley has sprouted, it likes cool temperatures. Partially shaded areas are preferred. In a greenhouse when there are long days of sun, a shade cloth set-up would be nice for the parsley plants.

Before transplanting the seedlings into your garden, harden them off a week beforehand. Set them outside for an hour or two at a time, increasing the amount of time as you go. This helps the seedlings acclimate to the outdoor temperature and climate.

Parsley will be ready to harvest ten-twelve weeks after being planted. Snip the leafy stems off at the base to harvest. The leaves will grow many more times.

DILL

Dill is a bi-annual that prefers warm temperatures. In most regions, it is grown as an annual. Grow dill in containers and raised beds. It's not recommended to plant it in the ground because it might self-seed all over the greenhouse (if you don't harvest the dill seeds in time).

To germinate, dill needs soil temperatures between 60 and 70°F (16-21C). Sow seeds in April or May, when the soil is warm enough. Dill doesn't transplant well, so it's best not to do seed starts. Some dill varieties grow pretty large, 2-4 feet (60-121cm) high, so look for dwarf varieties if you're going to keep it in the greenhouse. Or consistently pinch off the tops to keep the plant contained.

Sow dill seeds every 2-3 weeks during spring for a continuous harvest. Plant them ¼" (.6cm) deep and 18 inches (45cm) apart. The seeds will sprout in 10-14 days. Once the plants are 2-3 inches (2-8cm) tall, thin them to 12-18 inches (30-45cm) apart. Pinch the flowers off before they bloom to keep the plants producing new foliage.

MINT, LEMON, BALM, CATNIP

These perennials, all in the mint family love light and warmth but aren't overly picky about where they grow. Only grow mint species in containers as it has a habit of spreading intrusively if not kept contained. Mint multiplies by roots, so it's essential they aren't allowed to spread out.

Move plants outdoors during the summer and then back into the greenhouse in fall. Mint plants in cool climates will eventually die back, and you can cut the stems 2" (5cm) above the base and set the containers in a corner. In spring, when it warms up again, give them a little water, and they'll sprout up.

You can grow mint from seeds or starts, but it's much easier to get starts. Mint seed grows slowly. To keep the mint plants producing, cut them back to 1" (2.5cm) above the ground right before they start flowering. New leaves will sprout up soon, and it's possible to get 2-3 harvests in one season. Many mints, lemon balm, and catnip species grow quite tall, so choose a dwarf variety or keep a pair of pruning shears nearby. On the plus side, you'll never run out of mint! There are tons of mint varieties available, including chocolate mint and pineapple mint, making this a fun and fruitful greenhouse choice.

OREGANO

Oregano does well as a perennial in zones 5 and above. It will need good winter mulching to make it through the winter though. Plant oregano in containers so they can be moved around as needed, or plant in raised beds that can be covered in winter. Oregano likes hot weather, no prolonged frosts, and minimal watering.

Keep oregano in the greenhouse or take it outdoors to enjoy the sunshine in the summer. Then, when it starts getting cool, move it inside again. Cut the plants back to 2" (5cm) tall and cover the pots with 4-6 inches (10-15cm) of soil and mulch. This is to keep the roots as warm as possible. Place the pots of oregano in full sunlight. Oregano is best started from cuttings or as a transplant in late May or June when all danger of frost is gone. It does not grow reliably from seed. Oregano plants average 1-2 feet (30-60cm) tall but can be easily kept to a smaller size with regular pruning.

After you've overwintered your oregano plants, wait until the room temperatures get to be above 65°F (18C), and then uncover the pots and water the plants. New growth will appear soon.

A perennial that does best in hot, dry climates, rosemary can be grown in the greenhouse but may need special care during the winter. Plant it in containers that can be moved around easily to suit the herb's needs.

ROSEMARY

There are new rosemary cultivars on the market today that will survive in USDA zone 6 temperatures, but only a few. Most varieties need warmer climates.

To keep rosemary surviving throughout the winter, place the plants in a warm sunny location in the greenhouse. This isn't to keep them growing foliage, as that will likely cease or slow, but it is essential to keep the roots warm enough, so the plants don't die completely.

Cut back the growth to 3" (7.5cm), then, after the first frost, bury the plants with soil and mulch to keep them warm. Use 4-6 inches (10-15cm) of soil and mulch, and if you're in an especially cold location, add another layer with a frost blanket. If this isn't enough, you can also bring the containers into the house with you, where it is likely warmer with more light.

During the summer season, rosemary is fine

staying in the greenhouse or moving outdoors. Just make sure you don't leave it outside when it gets cold. Full-grown plants grow up to 4-feet (1.2m) tall, so keep that in mind. This only happens in climates where it doesn't die back from the cold.

Rosemary is best acquired as a potted herb; it's challenging to sow from seed. Always locate rosemary plants in full sun..

SAGE AND THYME

Both sage and thyme are cold-hardy perennials that die back in winter in cold climates. Start with small plants or stem cuttings from a gardening friend. Neither of these herbs germinates reliably from seed. Start them in the greenhouse after all danger of frost has passed.

Thyme is resilient down to USDA zone 4 while sage is hardy to zones 5 and up. These herbs are on the smaller size – thyme averages 6-12 inches (1.2m) tall, while sage grows 12-30 inches (30-76cm) tall. Of course, size is dependent on variety. And you can keep them both smaller with regular pruning.

It's best to keep them in containers that can be moved in and out of the greenhouse based on weather and temperature. However, both can also be directly planted in the greenhouse. Don't forget they're there, and they'll return every year in the same spot.

To overwinter, move any containers to the greenhouse after the first frost. Cut the plants down to 2" (5cm), place them in a sunny location, and cover them with 4-6 inches (10-15cm) of mulch or compost to keep the roots warm. Once the temperature in the greenhouse reaches a consistent 60°F (16C) in spring, remove the mulch and water the plants. They will resprout soon.

ONIONS POTATOES AND GARLIC

Onions

Instead of relying solely on onion starts, plant seeds in January to give the bulbs a head start. Onion seeds don't mind the cold; they won't sprout until it warms up, but this early planting gives the seeds the cold stratification necessary to their growth and sets them up to be ready and eager for sprouting at the first sign of spring.

The key to successful onion starting from seed is to give them enough time to reach maturity before it gets hot. Onions are slow growers and prefer cooler weather – they will stop growing in the heat of summer. Starting them in January puts the seeds in the natural day-night cycle right from the beginning and results in them being triggered to grow at precisely the right time.

Plant intermediate or long-season onion seeds in a container with drainage holes and a lid. Repurposing an old plastic produce clamshell or a milk jug cut in half is perfect for this. Make holes in the bottom if there aren't any. Fill the container with several inches of potting soil, then sprinkle the onion seeds on top. Cover the seeds with ½ inch (1.27cm) of soil and water thoroughly. Place the lid on top and put the container in the greenhouse.

Don't worry about watering or cold; the cover allows some humidity to develop and keeps the seeds comfortable. If your greenhouse is heated, place the container in a shady location outdoors where it won't be bothered by critters.

When spring arrives, start opening the lid on warm days and then closing it again at night. Cover the container with a towel for extra insulation if there is a hard freeze coming.

In spring, when the onion seeds germinate, remove the lid and let the seedlings grow. Water as needed until the seedlings are 3" (7.5cm) tall. When they reach 3" (7.5cm), trim the tops off (they make an excellent snack or salad ingredient!).

Top trimming forces the onions to focus their energy on growing a bulb instead of green foliage. Trim the tops again in a month.

As soon as the ground is workable, transplant onions outside or to raised beds in the greenhouse. Onions are ready for harvesting when the tops turn brown and fall over.

Potatoes

February is the month to begin chitting the first batch of potatoes for planting in March. Chitting is simply pre-sprouting the tubers before planting to give the plants an extra head start. Only use seed potatoes (none from the grocery store – those have been treated with chemicals to prevent sprouting) and choose an early or mid-season variety.

Place the seed potatoes in a cool, frost-free location indoors with lots of light and the end with the most "eyes" facing upwards. In 6 weeks, the potatoes should have 1-2 inch (2.5-5 cm) long sprouts.

In March, cut the chitted potatoes into quarters or sections, with at least one strong sprout on each one. Let the cut sides heal over for 2-3 days, and then they're ready for planting. Plant them in large grow bags in the greenhouse or in raised beds. The grow bags will require a bit of room, so make sure there is plenty of space for them.

CHOOSING SEED VARIETIES FOR THE GREENHOUSE GARDEN

Some varieties thrive better in cold or hot temperatures than others. For example, some types of lettuce are developed to withstand cooler weather, while others have been cultivated to withstand heat. Be sure to read the seed packets and choose varieties that suit the conditions. Pick vegetable varieties that will do well in the temperature one to two months after planting – this is when the plants will be maturing and need either cold or heat tolerance, depending on where you live.

Potatoes are susceptible to frost – depending on the March climate conditions, you may need to warm the greenhouse at night or cover the plants with mulch. Potatoes take 45-70 days to mature, depending on the variety. Greenhouse started potatoes mature a month or more ahead of garden planted ones.

Do another chitting and planting a month later for consecutive potato harvests. Start another group in September for a fall harvest. Make sure the type you choose will have time to mature before the weather slows growth and tuber development.

Garlic

Garlic bulbs take approximately 8-10 months to mature to harvest. They are planted in the fall before the ground freezes, then harvested in July or August.

There are two varieties of garlic; hardneck and softneck. Both prefer cooler weather, but softneck is more tolerant of warm weather. Only plant garlic from seed cloves from a trusted source – grocery store varieties are often chemically treated so they won't sprout.

Plant garlic in the ground, in wide containers, or raised beds. Just be aware that the space in the raised bed will then be occupied for the next eight months. Pots or planting directly in the ground are the best options. Garlic requires a long cold season to germinate.

PLANTING PERENNIALS IN THE GREENHOUSE

Perennials are plants that remain in the soil year-round. Most people think of greenhouses as transitional spaces, where seeds are started before they are eventually transferred to the outdoor garden. However, if you have enough space in the greenhouse, it's nice to have some permanent plants in there, especially herbs.

Mint, thyme, chives, oregano and lemon balm are perennials that will stay green and viable longer in a greenhouse than outdoors. They will die back at some point, then resprout in the spring. Mint and lemon balm are known spreaders, so never plant them directly in the greenhouse dirt – keep them in a pot.

Having these herbs in the greenhouse extends their season at both ends. If you cover them with a cloche or hoop frame, they'll last even longer than when left uncovered.

Parsley and cilantro are semi cold-hardy biennials. They'll need some extra warmth and may drop off production during the coldest times, but then will come back in spring. But, having them in the greenhouse greatly extends their season, meaning you'll be enjoying fresh parsley well into November.

THE PROS AND CONS OF SUPPLEMENTAL LIGHTING & HEAT

Greenhouse growing doesn't need to slow down in winter if you can keep the temperatures above 45°F (7C) and provide 8-10 hours of light. Root vegetables and leafy greens do well in this situation. A greenhouse using supplemental light and ensuring nighttime temperatures above 62°F (17C) can grow tomatoes, peppers, and other warm-season crops. Whether this is a good choice for you or not depends on where you live and how much you want to spend on electricity. Keeping a greenhouse consistently warm during these times can really add up if you're heating it every night.

Chapter 6

SPACE UTILIZATION
& Companion Planting

USING SPACE EFFECTIVELY

The way you set up your greenhouse will depend entirely on what size and type of greenhouse you have. There is no right or wrong way, but here are some tips for making the space work well for you. Greenhouse space is finite, and it is highly recommended that you draw out a plan before you start putting anything in it.

Make space for a walkway or paths between your benches, shelves, raised beds or whatever growing containers you intend to use. You should be able to access every plant in the greenhouse within arm's reach. If plants are out of your reach, it will be extremely difficult to care for them properly. Do not sacrifice paths for more growing space. Having more growing space is great, but if you can't tend to the plants, check them for diseases, see if they are getting watered properly and so forth, it will be wasted.

ALWAYS HAVE A PLAN

- What plants will you be growing?
- How much space will each plant need?
- When will they be transplanted if that is the intention?
- What resources will each plant need?
- Can certain plants be grouped to conserve resources?

Not having a plan will leave you frustrated and running in circles. Deciding last minute how to deal with plants that grew bigger than anticipated, plants that are ready before you are and the like, takes a lot of the fun out of gardening.

Have some temporary tables on hand for those times when extra space is desperately needed. They can be set up and taken down easily and are relatively inexpensive. A table set up outside the greenhouse to hold extra containers, tools, and soil is very helpful.

Shelves can be set up for staging. This means keeping some plants on the lower shelves while you wait for the ones on the upper shelves to mature. This doesn't work with all plants, so plan accordingly.

Divide your greenhouse into zones if possible. With a very small greenhouse, this may be difficult. Zones will assist you in managing the space more effectively. One area of the greenhouse can be for all the shade-loving plants, and there can be shade cloths arranged over the glazing in that area. This will help you stay organized. It will also help to know where all your plants are, so you don't have to go searching for specific ones in the multitude of plants surrounding you.

Use hooks, hanging baskets, and other wall and ceiling attachments to utilize the vertical space around you. Tools can be hung on hooks. Plants can go in baskets. This can greatly increase the available space in your greenhouse.

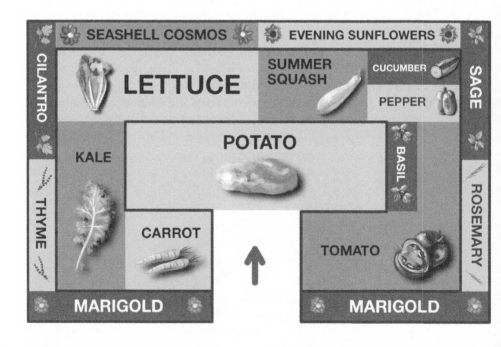

COMPANION PLANTING

Companion planting in the greenhouse is a bit different from the outdoor garden. If you're just using the greenhouse to do seed starts, companion planting isn't necessary because all the seedlings will eventually be moved outside.

Usually, companion planting is done to reduce pests, improve harvests, provide support structures, better use space, and prevent weeds. In a greenhouse, companion planting works only with the vegetables, herbs, fruits, and flowers that are staying inside throughout their maturity. This means, depending on how you are using your greenhouse, companion planting may not be worthwhile.

Attracting pollinators and beneficial insects is a great reason to companion plant in a greenhouse. Greenhouses naturally have fewer insects because they're more enclosed. Growing flowers and vegetables that draw them in will greatly improve your crops by improving pollination and eliminating pests.

In southern greenhouses, larger plants, such as tropical bananas or tall vines, make excellent shade plants for tender seedlings below. This is a great way to naturally provide shade for young plants without sacrificing space. Tomatoes and eggplants are excellent shade plants, too, for smaller crops such as lettuce or spinach. The shaded greens will produce longer if they are protected from the heat and hot sun.

Pests are a common issue for greenhouse growers, and there are some plants that help with that. Nasturtiums attract aphids, so include a few in the greenhouse to keep the aphids away from your other plants. Sweet Alyssum is another flower that helps with aphid infestations as it attracts insects that eat aphids.

Dill, cilantro, and basil attract predatory insects, which will then naturally keep pest populations controlled. These herbs also attract pollinators. Dill and basil also protect plants from hornworms.

Marigolds attract whiteflies, a regular greenhouse pest for tomatoes. Grow marigolds, and the whiteflies will go to them instead of the tomato plants. Marigolds also attract bees, but you have to plant the simple marigolds, not super hybridized ones. Newer cultivated species of marigolds have much larger flower heads which aren't accessible to bees.

To learn more about which vegetables grow best together, and which ones should never be near each other, consult the Companion Planting Chart.

CUCUMBER

Friends	Foes
Beans	Aromatic
Cabbage	Herbs
Lettuce	Potatoes
Peas	
Radish	
Tomatoes	
Chives	
Corn	
Dill	
Kale	
Kohlrabi	
Marigolds	
Nasturtiums	
Onions	
Peppers	

PEPPERS

Friends	Foes
Eggplant	Beans
Onions	Broccoli
Tomatoes	Kale
Geranium	
Basil	
Carrot	

EGGPLANT

Friends	Foes
Beans	Fennel
Peppers	
Calendula	
Marigold	
Mint	
Peas	

POTATOES

Friends	Foes
Beans	Tomatoes
Cabbage	Pumpkin
Coriander	Cucumber
Marigold	Squash
Maize	Melons
Brinjal	Sunflowers

KALE

Friends	Foes
Onions	Peppers
Aromatics	Tomatoes
Dill	Squash
Sage	Beans
Rosemary	
Potatoes	
Beetroot	
Celery	
Garlic	
Geranium	

RADISHES

Friends	Foes
Peas	Kohlrabi
Lettuce	
Cucumber	
Beans	

TOMATOES

Friends	Foes
Cucumber	Cabbage
Onions	Corn
Peppers	Broccoli
Basil	Kale
Parsley	Potatoes
Chives	Fennel
Carrots	
Celery	
Calendula	
Geranium	
Borage	

ONIONS

Friends	Foes
Broccoli	Peas
Cabbage	Beans
Carrots	
Kale	
Lettuce	
Peppers	
Tomatoes	

BROCCOLI

Friends	Foes
Spinach	Peppers
Onions	Tomatoes
Dill	Squash
Sage	Pole Beans
Rosemary	
Potatoes	
Beetroot	
Celery	
Garlic	

PEAS

Friends	Foes
Carrots	Onions
Cucumber	Garlic
Radish	
Tomatoes	
Beans	

CARROTS

Friends	Foes
Beans	Dill
Onions	Strawberries
Lettuce	Fennel
Peas	Cabbage
Chives	
Leeks	
Rosemary	
Sage	

LETTUCE

Friends	Foes
Beets	Celery
Carrots	Parsley
Cabbage	
Cucumber	
Onions	
Radish	
Squash	
Strawberries	
Beans	

SQUASH

Friends	Foes
Lettuce	Broccoli
	Kale

BEANS

Friends	Foes
Radish	Onions
Eggplant	Peppers
Potatoes	Garlic
Cucumber	Fennel
Beets	Brassicas
Peas	
Strawberries	
Celery	
Corn	
Swish Chard	
Marigolds	
Sunflowers	

BEETS

Friends	Foes
Lettuce	Pale Beans
Bush Beans	Dill
Carrots	
Corn	
Cucumber	
Garlic	
Kohlrabi	
Leeks	
Onion	

TURNIPS

Friends	Foes
Peas	Eggplant

THE BEGINNER'S GUIDE TO GREENHOUSE GARDENING *Richard Bay*

HYDROPONICS IN A GREENHOUSE

Turning a greenhouse into a hydroponics growing space can be done quite easily. And, without costing a fortune either. It will take a little adjustment in space and growing techniques, but it is not difficult.

Greenhouse growing is all about controlling the environment around you to create the best possible situation so plants can thrive. Hydroponics has that same goal. Combining the two creates the best of both worlds and makes an amazing space for plants to grow quickly and vigorously.

Basically, the greenhouse can become the dedicated space for growing hydroponically. All six hydroponic systems can be set up in a greenhouse. There will need to be some rearranging and re-purposing of space, but other than that, it won't take much. Hydroponics requires lighting and heating methods just like greenhouse gardening. The humidity and climate need to be controlled carefully to protect the plants in both situations.

The cost of growing hydroponically in the greenhouse is less than growing with soil. The soil needed to grow vegetables adds up fast when you're planting large quantities. Hydroponics eliminates that cost entirely. A hydroponic garden that is not in a greenhouse must use a lot of electricity to make sure there is adequate light and heat for the plants. A greenhouse provides a lot of heat and light naturally from the sun which makes the cost of growing hydroponically less expensive too. Like regular greenhouse gardening, the only time you will need to supplement heat or light is during cool months with shorter days.

A greenhouse will need access to electricity and have an external heat source (other than the sun) to be conducive for hydroponic growing. A tunnel greenhouse or hoop house won't work; however, an A-frame, dome, post, and rafter or attached greenhouse would make a great location for hydroponics.

Plants that do well in a hydroponic greenhouse are tomatoes (they thrive!), lettuce, mint, basil, cabbage, strawberries, and green beans. Plants that take up a lot of room, like pumpkins or any melon, will not work well in a greenhouse with its limited space.

A hydroponic greenhouse can not only extend your growing season, but it can increase your productivity. Plants growing in soil take longer to mature.

MANAGING & OPERATING

a greenhouse

The health and productivity of your greenhouse depends on thorough and efficient management. Creating optimal growing conditions for a variety of plants with a wide variance of needs can get complicated. It isn't difficult, yet without planning, it can be chaotic. Chaos breeds mistakes and it is the plants you are trying to grow that will suffer. Plants can get forgotten or be placed into climate situations which aren't good for them if there isn't the appropriate planning.

Creating and keeping a schedule of what you are growing, and the individual needs and growth schedules of each crop will make your greenhouse run smoothly and keep your plants happy and healthy.

CLEANING A GREENHOUSE

preparing for the next season

Greenhouses can become dirty places. After all, you are dealing with actual dirt. It's not just the inside that needs to be cleaned though. Glass windows need to be cleaned. If there are gutters, they will need to be cleaned out. Set aside at least one day a year to give the greenhouse a thorough cleaning. For greenhouses that are used only as season-extenders, clean them in the late fall after the growing season is done. For those that are used all year round, clean in the fall when there are mild temperatures. For periodically used greenhouses, clean them in-between uses.

A clean greenhouse is necessary for the health of the plants. Diseases can grow in dirty conditions. Pests can prosper. Dirty glazing will hinder the amount of light that comes in.

TO CLEAN A GREENHOUSE:

1. Remove all the plants to a protected area.

2. Take a broom or vacuum and remove all the debris from the floor.

3. Wash down all the structural parts of the greenhouse. Use a disinfectant or detergent that is not harmful to plants. There are specialty greenhouse cleaning solutions available.

4. Wash the inside and outside of the glazing materials. If it is plastic, test a small piece first to make sure you won't damage it. If you used shade paint, wash that off too.

5. Scrape out dirt between panes. A flexible plastic plant label works great for this.

6. Replace or fix anything that is broken.

7. Clean out the gutters if you have them.

Greenhouses are fragile in places so exercise caution, especially when cleaning the glazing and anyplace higher than your reach. Do not lean against walls. There are long handheld tools available to reach high places. Wear gloves and safety glasses if you are dealing with glass.
Before you start growing the next round of crops in your greenhouse, make sure all the systems are in working order. Assess all the vents to ensure they are opening and closing properly. Inspect the frame and glazing for cracks, chips, breaks, or anything else that will need to be repaired before you house plants in there again. Inspect your shade covers and purchase more if needed. Take inventory of your pots and tools to make sure there are enough and are the ones that you need. If you have a watering system, check it over for leaks or blockages. If there is a heating or cooling system, inspect it to make sure it will continue operating correctly. Take inventory of your insecticides, cleaning materials, soil, and other growing mediums to ensure there is enough.
Take a moment and evaluate the previous growing season. Is there anything you wished you had had at that time? Additional vents? Bigger pots? A different tool? Paver stones to walk on instead of gravel? Every year of greenhouse gardening is a year to learn new things. Take these lessons and apply them to the next year. Make the greenhouse work for you.

Chapter 7

PESTS & DISEASES

Cleanliness is the best way to prevent pests. Make sure any new plants that are brought into the greenhouse are pest and disease free. If any of them carries anything, it can quickly spread through the enclosed space of the greenhouse. If you see any plants with pests or disease, immediately remove them from the greenhouse. A good plan is to place any new plant outside the greenhouse for a few days as quarantine before bringing it inside.

Mesh should be placed over all ventilation openings to reduce the chance of pests entering the greenhouse. Any crack or holes that appear in the walls should be attended to immediately.

Greenhouses are great because they do eliminate a lot of potential pests and infestations that occur outside. However, that is a double-edged sword because often outside there are predators that eat and help fend off pests. When the balance of nature is changed, these predators are no longer there to help us, and so we need to tackle the problems differently. The majority of insects and pests reproduce at a fast rate, and a small infestation can quickly become a huge one. Check your plants frequently. Pay close attention to any signs of distress. Look under leaves and on stems. The type of pest or disease that shows up in your greenhouse will depend on your location and what you are growing; however, there are a few common ones to watch out for.

THRIPS

These tiny little pests require a multifaceted treatment approach. They are usually a yellowish-green color but can also be other colors. The larvae leave a shiny trail and teeny black specks of fecal matter on leaf surfaces. Blue sticky traps will combat the adults who fly around. An insecticide for soft-bodied insects will take care of the larvae and eggs on the plant.

APHIDS

These little tear-shaped bugs are found on the undersides of leaves. They can be green, brown, black, yellow and pink. Signs of an aphid infestation include wilting and generally unhealthy-looking plants. An insecticide

THE BEGINNER'S GUIDE TO GREENHOUSE GARDENING *Richard Bay*

specifically for soft-bodied insects works well to get rid of them.

WHITEFLIES

These look like little white moths and will fly around when the foliage is disturbed, making them easy to identify. In small numbers, they aren't harmful to the plants, but if left on their own, they will multiply and become a problem. They leave a shiny residue on leaves that will turn into black mold if it builds up too much. Sticky traps are good for catching the adults. An insecticide for soft-bodied insects will take care of the eggs and larvae.

MEALYBUGS

These bugs create easily identifiable cotton ball-like masses in the joints of plants. They drink the sap of leaves and stems causing plants to wilt and leaves to turn yellow. An insecticide for soft-bodied insects will take care of them. Continue treatment even after it looks like they are gone. They often reappear weeks and months later.

SPIDER MITES

If you see little yellow specks all over your plants, you have a spider mite infestation. There may also be webbing between the branches and leaves. A miticide is needed to get rid of these pests. Treat the plants for at least a month because spider mite eggs are notoriously hard to destroy, and they will hatch even after being sprayed.

FUNGUS

Overly wet conditions can cause a variety of fungal diseases such as powdery mildew, botrytis, root rot, and phytophthora. All plants should have good drainage to prevent these diseases. Signs of a fungal infection are wilted plants, yellowing, collapse, or development of fuzzy growths on the leaves and stems. Fungal diseases can be treated with neem oil. Some plants can't be treated with neem oil so do your research before using it.

BACTERIAL DISEASE

These diseases are incurable. Signs include plant tissue looking like it is melting and turning into a sticky mess and water-soaked spots. Any plants showing these signs need to be immediately removed from the greenhouse and destroyed. Bacterial diseases are spread through dirty containers, tools, and clothing. A clean greenhouse with plenty of air circulation is the key to preventing these diseases.

VIRUSES

There are many types of viruses. The most common symptom is yellow rings or a mosaic pattern on leaves. Viruses are usually brought in by insects and pests, which is another reason to treat any pest infestations immediately and thoroughly. Viruses are not treatable, and any plants showing signs need to be removed from the greenhouse and destroyed.

GETTING STARTED

Having a greenhouse can be very rewarding. It is a useful tool and can enhance any garden. The possibilities that a greenhouse can provide are numerous. From a small, portable, fold-up, greenhouse to a large, heated, permanent one, the potential for greater garden production is endless. If you're not sure how much you will use a greenhouse, start with a small, non-permanent one and see how you like it. There is always a learning curve with new things, so don't be disheartened if it doesn't go perfectly. Every greenhouse situation is different, and even master gardeners can run into unexpected problems. So keep experimenting and most importantly have fun with your greenhouse!

For those who want to dive deeper into gardening practice, check out the free bonus. Here you'll get some handy tips on how you can use companion planting strategies to get the most out of your garden. Also, you will find some advice on how to save seeds for upcoming growing seasons. All you need to do is to enter the URL below and download the PDF:

https://greenhousebonus.gr8.com/

ABOUT THE AUTHOR

Richard's father was a keen gardener and that is where his interest in all natural things began. As a youngster, he enjoyed nothing better than helping his father in the garden.

Nowadays, he finds himself at the opposite end of life. Having had a satisfying career, he now has time to potter around in his garden and take care of his small homestead. Much of the food on his dinner table is homegrown. He likes to experiment with various gardening methods and find new ways to grow bountiful crops year-round.

He wants to share his knowledge showing how easy and rewarding it is to set up your own prosperous garden. In his opinion, you do not need a huge budget to get started. When you do get started, you will soon feel, and taste, the benefits of growing your own food.

Learn more about Richard Bray at

https://www.amazon.com/author/richardbray

Made in the USA
Coppell, TX
01 April 2023

15024876R00088